TABLE OF CONTENTS

Chapter 1: Introduction ....

Chapter 2: A Brief MVC Overview 9

Chapter 3: Setting up The Development Environment 13

Chapter 4: Adding a Controller 27

Chapter 5: Working With Views 35

Chapter 6: Working With Models 47

Chapter 7: Connecting up to a database 53

Chapter 8: Retrieving a recipe from the database and viewing it 67

Chapter 9: Adding A Search Facility 75

Chapter 10: Extending the Model 87

Chapter 11: Adding The Create Recipe Functionality 91

Chapter 12: Adding Edit Functionality 103

Chapter 13: Adding Delete Functionality 113

Chapter 14: Finishing Touches 123

Chapter 15: Final Word 125

ASP.NET MVC using .NET 8 - Getting Started with a Small Project using SQLite and Entity Framework

Ian Preston

Copyright © 2024 Ian Preston

All rights reserved.

Copyright © 2024 by Ian Preston

All rights reserved.

No part of this book may be reproduced in any form or by any electronic or mechanical means including information storage and retrieval systems, without permission in writing from the author. The only exception is by a reviewer, who may quote short excerpts in a review.

First Edition: April 2024

PREFACE

About this book

In this book, I'm going to attempt to take you on a hands-on, pragmatic, enjoyable journey to learn how to program Asp.Net MVC projects using .NET Core 8, SQLite and the Entity Framework. You'll be taking the steps required to start building your first project within minutes. Every chapter is designed to improve your understanding of the MVC framework, so once you've finished the book, you can begin to design and implement your own projects using Microsoft Asp.Net Core MVC , SQLite and the Entity Framework.

In the course of this book, we will cover:

- Chapter 1: Introduction
- Chapter 2: A Brief MVC Overview
- Chapter 3: Setting up The Development Environment
- Chapter 4: Adding a Controller
- Chapter 5: Working With Views
- Chapter 6: Working With Models
- Chapter 7: Connecting up to a database
- Chapter 8: Retrieving a recipe from the database and viewing it
- Chapter 9: Adding A Search Facility
- Chapter 10: Extending the Model
- Chapter 11: Adding The Create Recipe Functionality
- Chapter 12: Adding Edit Functionality
- Chapter 13: Adding Delete Functionality
- Chapter 14: Finishing Touches
- Chapter 15: Final Word

The goal of this book is to teach you how to program Asp.Net projects in a manageable way without overwhelming you. We will focus only on the essentials and cover the material in a hands-on, practical manner so that you can code along.

Working Through This Book

This book is purposely broken down into manageable chapters where the development process of each chapter will center on different essential topics. The book takes a practical, hands-on approach to learning through practice. You learn best when you code along with the examples in the book.

Requirements

No previous knowledge of Asp.Net development is required, but you should have basic programming knowledge. It will be a helpful advantage if you have some experience coding in Microsoft .Net, but even if you have not done so, you should still be able to follow along.

Getting Book Updates

To receive updated versions of the book, subscribe to our mailing list by emailing ian@hardworkingnerd.com. I will try to update my books to use the latest software and libraries and will update the code samples and content in this book. So, do subscribe to my list to receive updated copies!

Code Examples

You can obtain the source code of the completed project by emailing ian@hardworkingnerd.com

Acknowledgements

Thanks to all those who helped me in the writing of this book.

CHAPTER 1: INTRODUCTION

Welcome to ASP.NET MVC using .NET 8 - Getting Started with a Small Project using SQLite and Entity Framework! This book focuses on the key tasks and concepts to get you started to learn and build Asp.Net MVC applications at a faster pace. It is designed for readers who don't need all the details about everything inside the Asp.Net MVC stack at this point in the learning curve but want to concentrate on what you really need to know.

So what's the ASP.NET Core MVC framework? ASP.NET Core MVC is a popular framework developed by Microsoft for building modern, cross-platform web applications. It combines the power of the .NET Core platform with the Model-View-Controller (MVC) architectural pattern:

- .NET is a comprehensive coding framework created by Microsoft that has been widely used since the late 1990s. It provides a robust set of libraries and tools for developing various types of applications. In recent years, Microsoft introduced .NET Core, an open-source and cross-platform version of the .NET framework. .NET Core allows developers to build and run applications on multiple operating systems, including Windows, macOS, and Linux.

- MVC is a development pattern that aims to separate the code into three main components: Models, Views, and Controllers. This separation helps to keep the codebase organized, maintainable, and easier to test. We will look at the three concepts that make up the framework, models, views, and controllers a lot as the book goes on, so we won't go through them now.

By leveraging the MVC pattern, ASP.NET Core MVC enables developers to create scalable and maintainable web applications. The framework provides a set of conventions and helpers that simplify common tasks like routing, working with data, and handling user input.

The App We Will Be Building

We will build a Recipe database app that lets users save, view, and search for recipes. (Figures 1 and 2)

Figure 1 – Home Page with search functionality

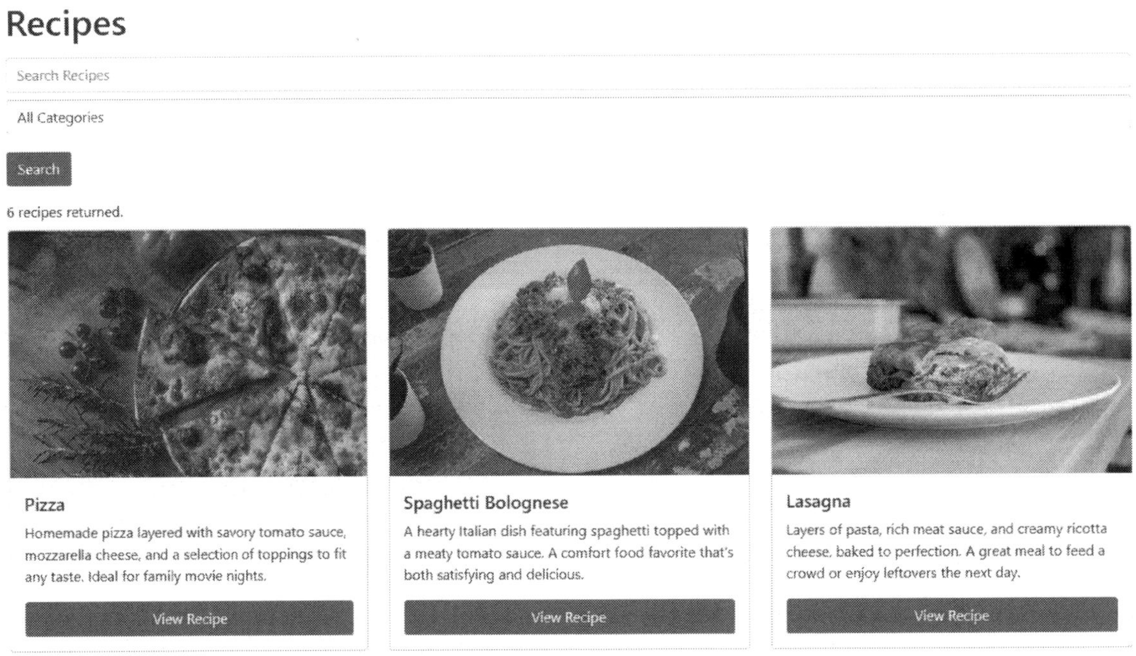

Recipes

Search Recipes

All Categories

[Search]

6 recipes returned.

Pizza
Homemade pizza layered with savory tomato sauce, mozzarella cheese, and a selection of toppings to fit any taste. Ideal for family movie nights.
[View Recipe]

Spaghetti Bolognese
A hearty Italian dish featuring spaghetti topped with a meaty tomato sauce. A comfort food favorite that's both satisfying and delicious.
[View Recipe]

Lasagna
Layers of pasta, rich meat sauce, and creamy ricotta cheese, baked to perfection. A great meal to feed a crowd or enjoy leftovers the next day.
[View Recipe]

Cheese Toastie

Category: Snacks

Description:
A luxurious sandwich fit for any meal

Instructions:
1. Preheat a skillet or griddle over medium heat.
2. Butter one side of each bread slice.
3. Place one slice of bread, butter side down, on the skillet.
4. Add the cheese slices on top of the bread in the skillet, covering the entire surface.
5. Place the second slice of bread on top of the cheese, butter side up.
6. Cook for 2-3 minutes, or until the bottom slice is golden brown and the cheese starts to melt.
7. Carefully flip the sandwich using a spatula and cook the other side for an additional 2-3 minutes, or until golden brown and the cheese is fully melted.
8. Remove the cheese toastie from the skillet and let it cool for a minute.
9. Cut the sandwich diagonally into two triangles.
10. Serve hot and enjoy your delicious cheese toastie!

[Edit This Recipe] [Delete This Recipe]

Figure 2 – Recipe details page

Users can see the list of recipes in the database, they will also be able to search for recipes and edit and delete recipes that are in the database.

We will first briefly examine the MVC framework and how Microsoft has implemented it for .Net Core/Asp.Net. We will then set up our development environment; part of this process will involve setting up a skeleton app that Microsoft provides. This will help to solidify our understanding of how an MVC project fits together.

We will then write some code to firm up our understanding of the Model, View, and Controller concepts. Finally, we will use what we have set up and learned in the previous chapters to begin coding our recipe database app.

Chapter 2: A Brief MVC Overview

MVC stands for Model, View, Controller. It's a general term for an architectural pattern used extensively in software development and is not just confined to the Asp.Net space.

The Model-View-Controller (MVC) framework was devised to combat "spaghetti code," a term used to describe disorganized and tangled code that is difficult to follow and manage, like a plate of spaghetti. Spaghetti code often occurs in projects where the program's structure is unclear, leading to code that is hard to maintain, test, and modify.

What is spaghetti code?

Spaghetti code is characterized by:
- **Lack of structure**: The code lacks a clear, organized structure, making it hard to understand the relationships and dependencies between different program parts.
- **Tight coupling**: The code's components are heavily interdependent, which means changes in one area can unexpectedly affect others.
- **Lots of duplicate code**: Repeated code snippets scattered throughout the project can mean the same functionality is implemented in many different places. This means code changes need to be made in multiple places, and functionality can subtly differ in different parts of the app.

Issues with spaghetti code

While spaghetti code can sometimes be a quick solution, it tends to introduce several problems:
- **Hard to maintain**: Since the code isn't well-organized and components are interdependent, making even small fixes can be a challenge. This increases the risk of introducing new bugs while fixing old ones.
- **Hard to test**: Disorganized code makes it difficult to isolate parts for testing, complicating the testing process and making thorough testing nearly impossible.
- **Hard to make changes**: Modifying one part of the code often requires changes in many other areas to avoid breaking the application, making updates time-consuming and risky.

How MVC helps:

The MVC framework addresses these issues by dividing an application into three interconnected parts, each responsible for a specific aspect of the application. Specifically,

MVC splits things into three distinct sections

- Models
- Views
- Controllers

Let's discuss how each of these sections will be used in an asp.net MVC app

Models: In an ASP.NET MVC application, models represent the data and business logic of the application. In our example recipe database app, the models will define the structure and properties of each recipe.

Typically, models in an ASP.NET MVC app are implemented as classes with properties corresponding to the model's data fields. For example, a Recipe model might include properties such as Id, Title, Description, Ingredients, and Recipe Instructions.
Models can also include validation attributes to enforce data integrity and consistency. For instance, you might apply a *[Required]* attribute to the Title property to ensure that a recipe always has a title. Additionally, models can contain business logic related to the data they represent. For example, a Recipe model might have a method called *GetTotalCalories()* that calculates the total calories based on the ingredients (something like this would be way too advanced for our sample app though 🙂)

Views: Views display the model data to the user on the screen. They should not contain any complex business logic, but they may include some simple code for looping through a collection of model objects or conditionally showing certain properties based on specific criteria.

For example, a View might use a loop to iterate over a list of products returned by the Model and display each one with its name, image, and price. It may also have an if statement that only shows an item's discount price if it's currently on sale. The key is keeping the View code focused on presentation and rendering, not complex business logic or data manipulation.

One super useful feature of the ASP.NET MVC engine is the concept of a "master page." This lets you define a common skeleton or template for your web pages, which could include things like the header, navigation, and footer. Then, you can render your individual Views inside this master layout.

The big advantage of master layouts is that they allow you to make site-wide changes in one central place. So, if you want to update your header design or add a new menu item, you only have to modify the master layout file, rather than hunting through and editing every single View file. This saves a ton of time and keeps your site looking consistent.

Controllers: Controllers are the brains behind the operation of an ASP.NET MVC application. They act as a middleman between the Models and the Views, handling user input and deciding what to do with it. In our recipe database app, a Controller might take care of actions like adding a new recipe, updating an old one, or simply fetching all the recipes to display.

A typical Controller in an ASP.NET MVC app is implemented as a class with methods that respond to different HTTP requests. For example, you might have a method called *Create()* for adding new recipes, *Edit()* for updating an existing recipe, and *Recipes()* for listing all recipes. These methods interact with the Model to retrieve or save data, and then choose a View to display that data.

Controllers also handle the nitty-gritty of data transfer between the Models and Views. When a user submits a form to add a new recipe, the Controller's *Create()* method will receive the form data, use it to create a new Recipe model, and save it. If everything goes smoothly, it might redirect the user to the *Recipes* view to see the updated list of recipes. If there's an error (like missing a required title for the recipe), it might send the user back to the Create view with an error message.

The beauty of Controllers in MVC is that they help keep your code clean and organized. Each controller is responsible for a specific part of the application's functionality, which makes it easier to manage as your app grows. Plus, since the Controllers handle all the decisions and heavy lifting, your Views can stay simple and focused on presenting data, while your Models can stick to what they do best: dealing with data. This division of responsibilities makes your app easier to maintain and scale—no more spaghetti code here!

Routes: Although routes don't feature in the MVC acronym, they still play a key role in linking everything together. Imagine routes in your ASP.NET MVC application as tour guides that lead users to exactly where they need to go. When someone types a URL or clicks on a link, routes ensure they view the correct page, such as a detailed view of a recipe or a form to enter a new one.

Think of the recipe database app that we're going to implement. If someone wants to browse through a list of recipes, the routes ensure that the right controller and actions are called to gather and display that information. It's like having a map that matches URLs to various corners of your app.

Routes are set up to recognize patterns in the URLs and link them to specific actions in controllers. For instance, when you want to add a new recipe, there could be a straightforward URL like */Create* that the routes know should take you to the part of your app where you can input new recipe details. This makes URLs clean and easy to understand, almost like reading a simple sentence: go to */Create* to create a recipe.

Moreover, routes allow for customization to make links more intuitive. For example, instead of using complex and hard-to-remember URLs, you can set routes that allow URLs like */Recipes* to show all recipes or */Recipes/Edit* to edit an existing recipe. This helps keep your website easy to navigate, which is always a plus for users, and it also ensures it's easy for search engines such as Google to navigate and index your site.

Putting it all into action

All of this will start to make much more sense once we can see an MVC project in front of us, so in the next chapter we'll set up our development environment and create a skeleton app structure.

Following that, we'll review each letter in the MVC acronym and determine how it helps us implement our app. We'll then use the knowledge we have gained to start building our recipe database application.

Chapter 3: Setting up The Development Environment

Before we start implementing MVC in our recipe app, we'll set up a local development environment. I think it will be easier to see how the MVC framework fits together when we have some code in front of us.

In this book, we will be using Visual Studio Code to help us develop our recipe database app

Why are we using Visual Studio Code?

That's a good question! Both Visual Studio and Visual Studio Code are excellent IDEs (Integrated Development Environments) that make coding a lot easier and more efficient. However, for this project, I decided to go with Visual Studio Code, and here's why.

Visual Studio Code, or VS Code as it's often called, is incredibly versatile. It runs smoothly on Windows, Mac, and Linux systems, so no matter what computer you're using, you can follow along without any hitches. I really wanted this book to be as accessible as possible to everyone, regardless of the operating system they are using.

Another great thing about VS Code is that it's lightweight and fast. It doesn't take up much space on your computer, and it starts quickly, letting you jump right into your coding projects without a long wait. Plus, VS Code has a really active community and a vast library of extensions that you can use to customize it and enhance your coding experience.

If you're a fan of Visual Studio, that's totally fine, too! The good news is that you can adapt the exercises in this book for Visual Studio. Both IDEs share many similar functionalities, so transitioning between them isn't too tough. Visual Studio is a bit more feature-rich and tailored towards larger projects or enterprise solutions, which might be more than we need for the purposes of this book, but it's still perfectly capable of handling our exercises.

So, we're using Visual Studio Code because it's simple, effective, and works on any operating system, making our coding journey together as easy as possible. Whether you're a seasoned programmer or just starting out, VS Code is a reliable tool that should serve you well throughout this project.

Setting up the dev environment

The first thing we'll need to do is download the latest version of Microsft SDK; you can find the download here https://dotnet.microsoft.com/en-us/download. Once the SDK has been downloaded, install it on your machine.

After you've installed the SDK, it should be possible to check the correct runtime has been installed by issuing the command

```
dotnet --list-runtimes
```

From a command prompt on your machine

```
C:\Windows\system32\cmd.exe

Microsoft Windows [Version 10.0.19045.4170]
(c) Microsoft Corporation. All rights reserved.

C:\Users\Ian>dotnet --list-runtimes
Microsoft.AspNetCore.App 6.0.21 [C:\Program Files\dotnet\shared\Microsoft.AspNetCore.App]
Microsoft.AspNetCore.App 7.0.2 [C:\Program Files\dotnet\shared\Microsoft.AspNetCore.App]
Microsoft.AspNetCore.App 7.0.10 [C:\Program Files\dotnet\shared\Microsoft.AspNetCore.App]
Microsoft.AspNetCore.App 8.0.3 [C:\Program Files\dotnet\shared\Microsoft.AspNetCore.App]
Microsoft.NETCore.App 3.1.27 [C:\Program Files\dotnet\shared\Microsoft.NETCore.App]
Microsoft.NETCore.App 6.0.10 [C:\Program Files\dotnet\shared\Microsoft.NETCore.App]
Microsoft.NETCore.App 6.0.21 [C:\Program Files\dotnet\shared\Microsoft.NETCore.App]
Microsoft.NETCore.App 7.0.2 [C:\Program Files\dotnet\shared\Microsoft.NETCore.App]
Microsoft.NETCore.App 7.0.10 [C:\Program Files\dotnet\shared\Microsoft.NETCore.App]
Microsoft.NETCore.App 8.0.3 [C:\Program Files\dotnet\shared\Microsoft.NETCore.App]
Microsoft.WindowsDesktop.App 3.1.27 [C:\Program Files\dotnet\shared\Microsoft.WindowsDesktop.App]
Microsoft.WindowsDesktop.App 6.0.10 [C:\Program Files\dotnet\shared\Microsoft.WindowsDesktop.App]
Microsoft.WindowsDesktop.App 6.0.21 [C:\Program Files\dotnet\shared\Microsoft.WindowsDesktop.App]
Microsoft.WindowsDesktop.App 7.0.10 [C:\Program Files\dotnet\shared\Microsoft.WindowsDesktop.App]
Microsoft.WindowsDesktop.App 8.0.3 [C:\Program Files\dotnet\shared\Microsoft.WindowsDesktop.App]
```

Figure 1 - A list of the runtimes installed on a development machine

Because we are going to code our project using AspNetCore 8, we need to ensure that it has been installed. As you can see in Figure 1, it's the fourth line down in the information that the command gives us, with version number 8.0.3.

Now we have the framework in place, we'll need to install Visual Studio Code, you can download the latest version of the IDE here

https://code.visualstudio.com/download

Choose the correct version for your operating system and then follow the on-screen instructions to install the program.

Now that we have the IDE all installed, we need to install some Visual Studio Code extensions that will help us develop our application. To start this process, click the extensions button as shown in Figure 2

Figure 2 – The extension button

Once the extension window has opened, search for and find the C# extension; it should look similar to Figure 3. Install the C# extension by clicking the "Install" button

Figure 3 – The C# extension

As a bare minimum, you'll need the c# extension in order to develop the sample app. If you're open to installing more than one extension I would also recommend the following extensions

- .Net Install Tool - This extension simplifies the process of setting up .NET environments by guiding users through the installation of the .NET SDK, enabling efficient project creation and management directly within Visual Studio Code.
- The C# Dev Kit—This extension offers a comprehensive toolkit for C# development in Visual Studio Code. It provides advanced features such as code completion and debugging tools, which, in my experience, just make the coding process flow a bit smoother.

If you choose to install those two extensions, then the Installed section at the top of the Extensions window should look similar to Figure 4.

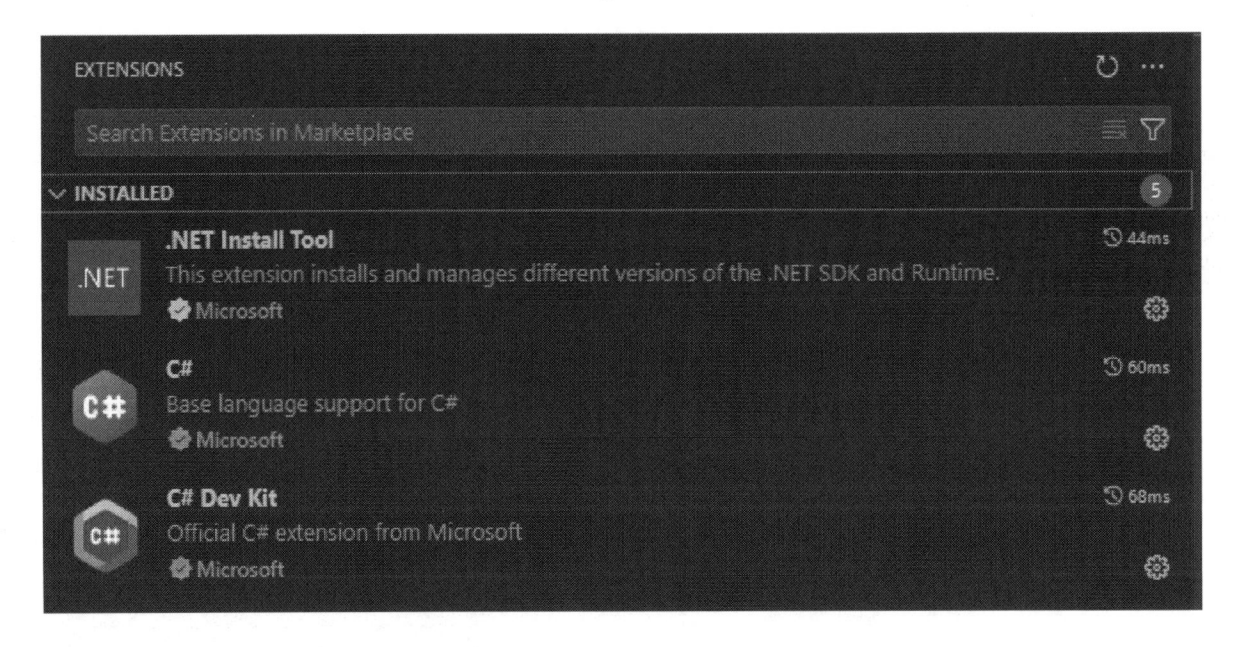

Figure 4 – your installed extension window should look similar to this

Now that we have the extensions set up, we need to create the project structure. Before we create the structure, create a folder on your machine to hold your projects. I'm going to create a folder in the C drive named "development projects."

Once you've created the folder, go to the File -> Open Folder menu option in Visual Studio Code and select it. If the VS code prompts you to ask if you trust the folder, confirm that you do.

Now, we need to create our project; Microsoft provides us with a base project template or "scaffold" that we can use. To create the project choose Terminal -> New Terminal from the VS Code menu and then enter the following command.

```
dotnet new mvc -n RecipeDatabase
```

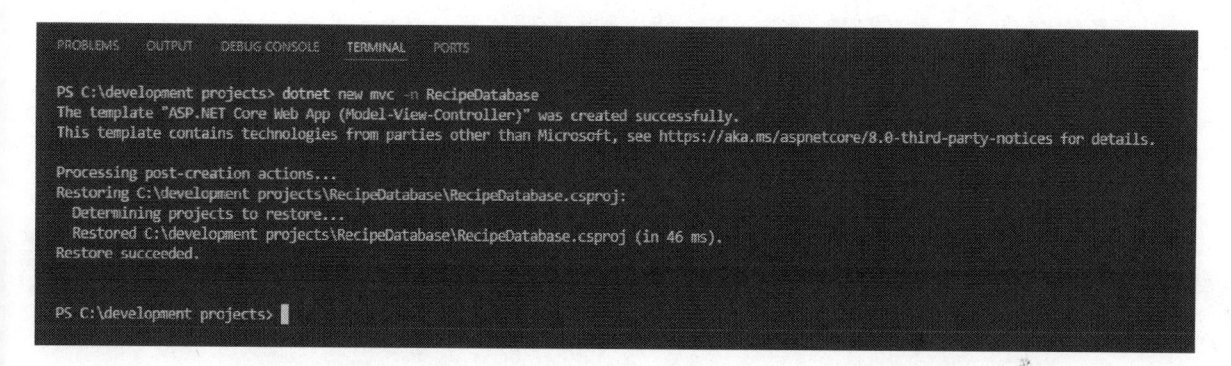

Figure 5 – running the dotnet project creation command in the terminal

Once the command has been run, it should create a folder named "RecipeDatabase" (this corresponds to the last argument we supplied to the command). You should be able to see the folder in the top left of the VS Code window. If you click the folder name then the project structure should expand

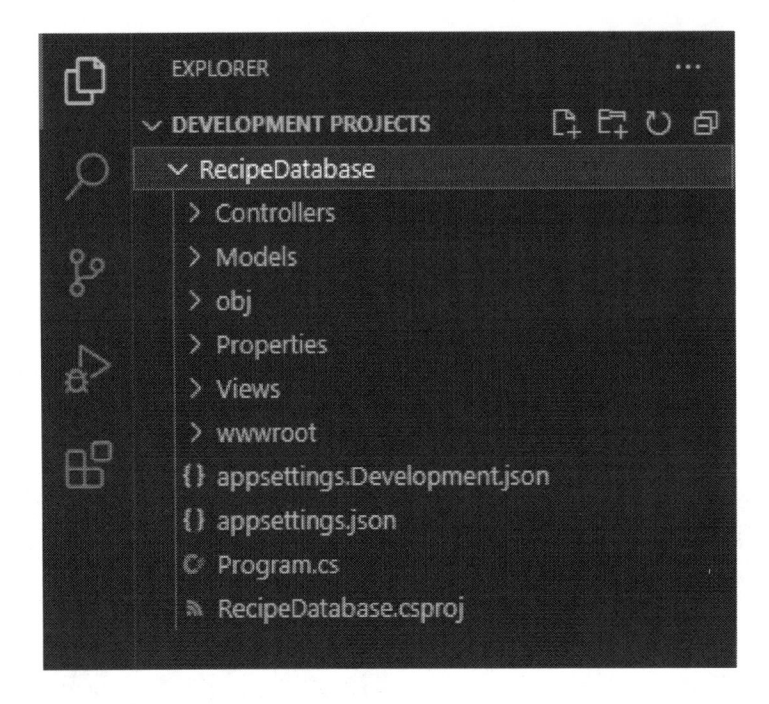

Figure 6 – the project files

Now we have our extensions set up, and the project files are in place, we need to get set up for debugging, to do this click the debug button in the left-hand side menu

Figure 7 - The debug menu button in the left hand-side menu

After you have clicked the debug button you should see something like Figure 8

```
         Run and Debug

To customize Run and Debug create
a launch.json file.

Show all automatic debug
configurations.

   Generate C# Assets for Build and
                Debug

To learn more about launch.json, see
Configuring launch.json for C#
debugging.
```

Figure 8 – Getting set up for debug

If you see the "Generate C# Assets for Build and Debug" button, then just go ahead and click it, but in my experience, the button isn't always there. If you can't see the button then follow these steps

- Open the command palette with **Ctrl+Shift+P**.
- Type and select **.NET: Generate Assets for Build and Debug**. This action creates a **.vscode** folder in your project directory if it doesn't already exist, containing two files: **launch.json** and **tasks.json**.

Once this is complete your project should be ready to run/debug and you should see a button similar to the one shown in Figure 9

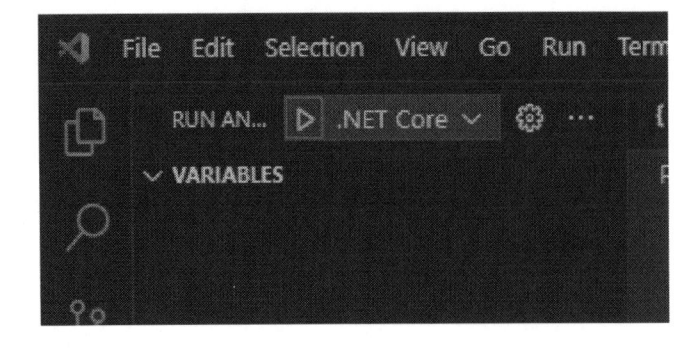

Figure 9– The green triangular debug button

If you click the button then the project should be launched in your default browser as seen in Figure 10

Figure 10 – The app start-up screen

If you look in the browser address bar in Figure 10, you can see that the site URL is https://localhost:7262. The 7262 value is a port number that is assigned by the web server that Visual Studio code uses to run the app. It's likely that the port number on your machine will be different. This won't cause any problems, but it's worth remembering that when I use URLs throughout the rest of the book, I'll be using the port number on my machine, so you will need to adjust them to reflect your port number.

You can change the port number by editing the Properties\launchSettings.json file in your project, but I would advise leaving it as is. You can see the JSON structure that holds the port numbers in Figure 11

```
11      "profiles": {
12        "http": {
13          "commandName": "Project",
14          "dotnetRunMessages": true,
15          "launchBrowser": true,
16          "applicationUrl": "http://localhost:5089",
17          "environmentVariables": {
18            "ASPNETCORE_ENVIRONMENT": "Development"
19          }
20        },
21        "https": {
22          "commandName": "Project",
23          "dotnetRunMessages": true,
24          "launchBrowser": true,
25          "applicationUrl": "https://localhost:7098;http://localhost:5089",
26          "environmentVariables": {
27            "ASPNETCORE_ENVIRONMENT": "Development"
28          }
29        },
30        "IIS Express": {
31          "commandName": "IISExpress",
32          "launchBrowser": true,
33          "environmentVariables": {
34            "ASPNETCORE_ENVIRONMENT": "Development"
35          }
36        }
37      }
38    }
```

Figure 11 – The port numbers listed in the launchSettings.json file

Once Visual Studio Code has launched the code in debug mode it will show a row of buttons near the top of the screen as shown in Figure 12

Figure 12 – The debugging buttons

These buttons can be used to navigate through the code whilst debugging, to end a debugging session click the red square button at the right of the button row

Stepping through the code

Visual Studio Code allows us to step through our source code, which can be very helpful when we're debugging. To test this functionality, go to the *HomeController.cs* file inside the Controllers folder. Find the *Index* action method and click to the left of the line number of the line of code that reads

return View();

a red dot should appear, as shown in Figure 13

Figure 13 – Setting a breakpoint

You can end any debug sessions you have running by clicking the red square button and start a new session by clicking the green triangular button.

As the code uses the Index function inside the Home Controller to render the home screen the code should pause at the breakpoint we set. It should look similar to Figure 14

Figure 14 – The code paused at a breakpoint

Once your breakpoint has been hit you can perform the following actions as shown in Figure 15

Figure 15 – The code navigation buttons

Clicking the blue triangle button (or pressing F5) will resume the code execution. This will run the code either to the next breakpoint or to its conclusion if no further breakpoints are encountered.

Clicking the arrow curled over the dot (or pressing F10) will navigate over the current line of code, so instead of diving into a function, the debugger will step over it (although it will still execute) and move on to the next line of code.

Clicking the arrow pointing at the dot (or pressing F11) will navigate into the function on the current line. The debugger will start stepping through the function's code on the current line and then return to the current line when the function has been stepped through.

Clicking the arrow pointing upwards from the dot (or pressing Shift + F11) will step out of the current function. The debugger will finish stepping through the current function and move to the line where it was called in its parent function.

Checking the project is using the correct .Net version

At the start of this chapter, we checked that .Net version 8 had been successfully installed; you can also check that your project is running on the correct .Net version by looking in the *RecipeDatabase.csproj* file at the root of your project

RecipeDatabase > RecipeDatabase.csproj

```
<Project Sdk="Microsoft.NET.Sdk.Web">

  <PropertyGroup>
    <TargetFramework>net8.0</TargetFramework>
    <Nullable>enable</Nullable>
    <ImplicitUsings>enable</ImplicitUsings>
  </PropertyGroup>

</Project>

```

Figure 16 – The DotNet version of the project

Auto Saving Your Work

By default, Visual Studio Code does not automatically save the changes you make to your code, if you prefer to work with autosaves then you can turn it in on near the bottom of the File menu as shown in Figure 17

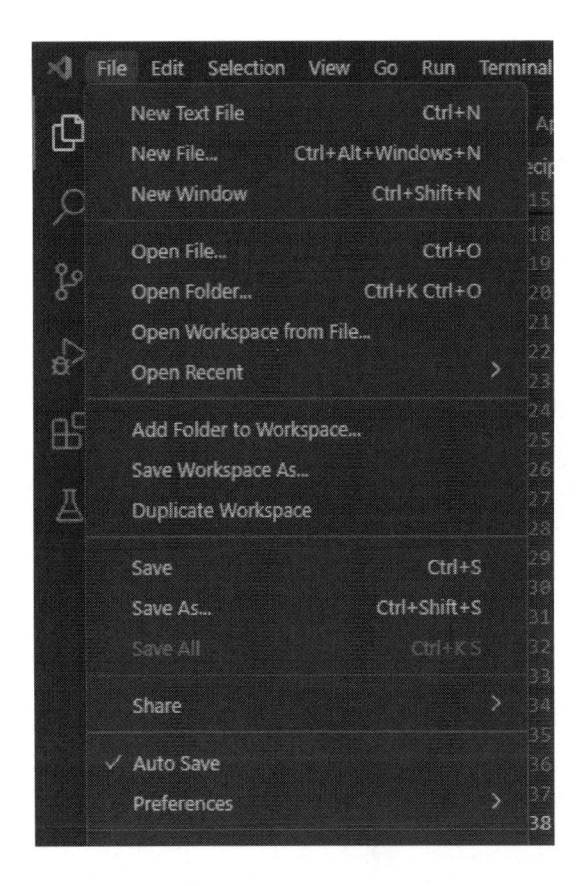

Figure 17 – Turning on autosaves

Whilst this will auto-save your work, it will not rebuild the project, so if you have made changes, it's always best to stop a debugging session using the red square button from the toolbar shown in Figure 12 and then restart it using the green triangle button

Common Issues

Hopefully, everything has gone swimmingly for you whilst setting up VS Code, but I've listed a few reasonably common errors below just in case you come up against them.

The language client requires VS Code version ^1.77.0 but received version 1.75.0

If you see an error like this, it is likely that your VS Code is out of date. Try navigating to Help -> Check for Updates... via the menus and check if there are any updates available.

Certificate Issues

VS Code will typically use a https certificate when it starts the site for a debug session, if you do see any certificate issues try running this command from the VS Code terminal

```
dotnet dev-certs https -trust
```

Key files and folders

As mentioned earlier in the chapter, after you've run the dotnet new MVC command, a set of predefined folders and files arranged in a helpful structure will be created in your project's *RecipeDatabse* folder. Let's walk through some of the key folders and files that you'll encounter:

The Controllers Folder

The Controllers folder is where all the controller classes are stored in your application. Controllers manage user requests, interact with models, and select appropriate views to display the response. Typically, each controller corresponds to a specific functionality or area of your application.

Using the MVC (Model-View-Controller) framework, all controllers are located within the Controllers folder. The framework follows the convention over configuration approach, which eliminates the need for unnecessary boilerplate code. To create a new controller, simply place a controller file in the Controllers folder and ensure that it inherits from the designated MVC Framework *Controller* class. The framework will automatically locate the controller when it needs to satisfy one of its root constraints. All that's required is to label the file as a controller and ensure it inherits correctly from the designated class.

The Views Folder

This folder contains your views, which are the templates used to generate the HTML content sent back to the client. The views in an MVC application are typically Razor files (.cshtml). They are organized into subfolders named after the controllers, making it easy to know which views correspond to which controller actions.

The views folder will typically hold folders for each of your controllers, and a shared folder that holds views that are likely to be used across the different controllers in your app.

The _Layout.cshtml File

Found in the Views/Shared folder, this Razor file defines a common site template (like a master page) that can be used across various views in your application to maintain a consistent look and feel. It typically includes things like the header, footer, and navigation menu. We'll discuss this view in greater detail in Chapter 5

The wwwroot Folder

This is where all the static files of your project live things like images, JavaScript files, and CSS stylesheets. Although the MVC framework uses a routing engine to resolve URLs, anything in this folder can be accessed directly. So, if the wwwroot folder contained a folder named images, with a file named burgers.jpg in it, we could access the file directly via this URL

https://localhost:7262/images/burgers.jpg

The wwwroot folder is the only folder in the project where you can access files like this, everything else needs to be accessed via the routing engine.

appsettings.json

This file contains configuration data, like connection strings for databases or application settings. It's a JSON file, making it easy to read and modify. You can have multiple versions of this file for different environments, such as appsettings.Development.json or appsettings.Production.json. When we add database functionality to the recipe app in Chapter 7 we will use this file.

Program.cs

This file is the starting point for the ASP.NET MVC application and you'll find it in the route of your project folder. It sets up important things like logging, routing, and overall application settings. Recently, Microsoft has updated this file to use fewer lines of code, making it simpler and easier to manage. We'll add to this file when we hook up to a database in Chapter 7.

Chapter 4: Adding a Controller

As this book progresses, we'll use controllers extensively to create our recipe database app. But before jumping in at the deep end, we'll add a simple controller to help us see how the controller and route functionality hang together.

Understanding Controllers and Actions

If you've done any C# programming before, it might help you to think of controllers as classes that handle web requests.

Inside the controller, we use functions (often called action methods) to respond to web requests and output content.

The Asp.Net framework provides a routing framework that allows us to map HTTP endpoints (or web addresses) to methods inside our controllers.

Don't worry if this sounds complex. We'll start with a simple example to make it easier to understand. Ready to see how a few lines of code can handle powerful web interactions? Let's dive in.

Creating a Simple Controller

Navigate to the Controllers folder in the RecipeDatabase project, right-click on the folder, and you should see a context menu appear (as shown in Figure 1)

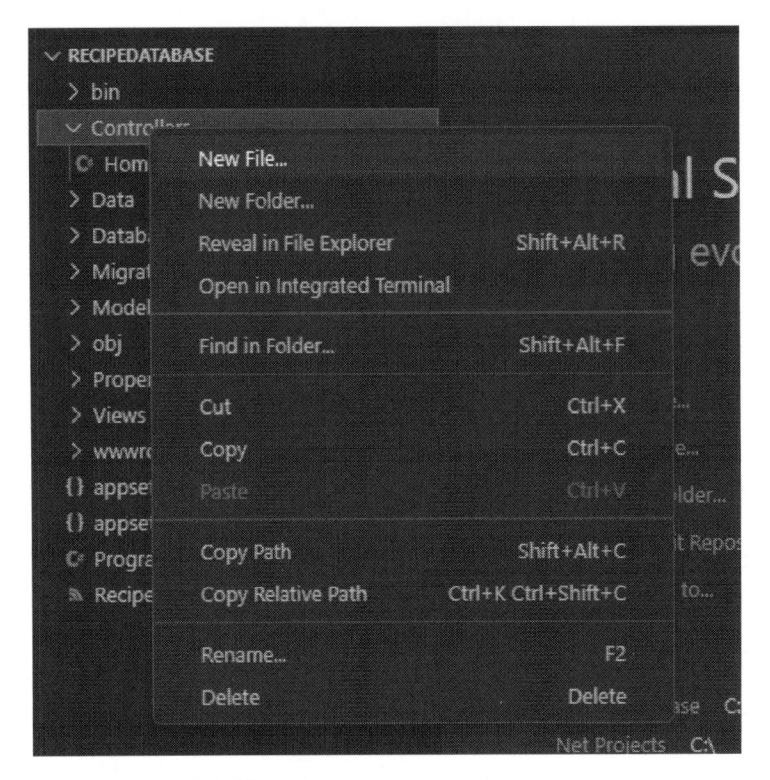

Figure 1 – The file menu

Select "New File" and create a file named "HelpController.cs"

Add the following code to the new file:

```csharp
using Microsoft.AspNetCore.Mvc;

namespace RecipeDatabase.Controllers
{
    public class HelpController : Controller {
        public IActionResult FAQ() {
            return Content("Hello! Here is the FAQ");
        }
    }
}
```

As you can see from the code, we define a class named HelpController that inherits from the Controller class. The Controller class is defined in the Asp.Net MVC framework, and inheriting from it informs the framework that our class can be used as a controller.

Inside the Controller, we define a function named *FAQ* with a return type of *IActionResult*. The function returns a string value via the I function, which is an Asp.Net MVC function that allows us to output content to the web response.

Once the code has been added to your project enter the Debug screen and click the triangular green triangle button to start debugging your project.

Once the website has appeared in your default browser, you should be able to see the content output by the controller using an address similar to this

https://localhost:7262/Help/FAQ

Once the webpage has loaded you should something like Figure 1

```
localhost:7262/Help/FAQ

Hello! Here is the FAQ
```

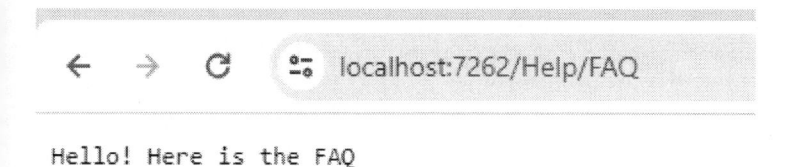

Figure 2 – The content being output to the screen

One of the first things you might notice about the webpage is that it does not render any of the top menu or styling that we saw when we first built the website in the previous chapter. This is because the homepage uses a view to render content to the screen, and as our FAQ method uses the *Content* function, it only renders the content that we supplied to it directly to the screen.

In the next chapter, we will examine the view engine in more detail and learn how to use it to render views.

When we entered https://localhost:7262/Help/FAQ into our browser's address bar, how did the framework find our controller and method? We can explain things by looking at the URL we entered section by section

1. The first section of the URL *https://localhost:7262* points to our ASP.NET MVC project, once the server has been successfully found, the routing engine gets to work

2. The second section of the URL *Help* points to our controller; by default, the MVC framework will try to find the value it finds in the second section of the URL to a controller. It does this by looking for any classes that inherit from the Controller class that are named <URLValue>Controller. In this case, it looks for a class named *HelpController* and finds the class that we added earlier.
3. Once the relevant controller has been found the MVC framework uses the third section of the URL, FAQ to search for a matching method inside the controller class, in this case, it finds our FAQ method and executes the code inside it, which returns the text we passed to the Content function in the response.

So why does the framework follow the steps above? Well, they're defined in the default route, which you can find in the *program.cs* file

```
app.MapControllerRoute(
    name: "default",
    pattern: "{controller=Home}/{action=Index}/{id?}");
```

As you can see from the code above the *app.MapControllerRoute* function takes a name argument and then a pattern argument that closely follows what was described above in the code. The pattern ignores the URL's host (the https://localhost:7262 bit) and then matches the first section of the URL to the controller, the second section to the action and anything following the second section to a parameter named id (we'll look at this in more detail below).

The pattern also supplies default values for the controller (where it supplies the value Home) and action (where it supplies the value Index) parts of the pattern, this is why, when you go to the web address

https://localhost:7262

The website will render the content returned by the *Index* action method on the *Home* controller.

What's happening with the id parameter?

If we look at the *app.MapControllerRoute* function again

```
app.MapControllerRoute(
    name: "default",
    pattern: "{controller=Home}/{action=Index}/{id?}");
```

We can see that the id section of the pattern is followed by a question mark, this is a Regular Expression convention that means that the id parameter might be there, but it also might not. This is why the Help and Home routes that we have tried so far work perfectly fine without the id parameter being present.

To use the id parameter let's rewrite our Help controller code, in the *HelpController.cs* file and the bold code below

```
using Microsoft.AspNetCore.Mvc;


namespace RecipeDatabase.Controllers
{
    public class HelpController : Controller {
        // Action to display a simple message
        public IActionResult FAQ(string id) {

            var idParameterText = " The id parameter was not supplied.";

            if (!string.IsNullOrEmpty(id)) {
                idParameterText = " The id parameter was supplied.";
                if (id == "carrot") {
                    idParameterText = " The id parameter was supplied, and it's value was carrot.";
                }
            }


            return Content("Hello! Here is the FAQ." + idParameterText);
        }
    }
}
```

Our updated code adds some functionality to accommodate the ID parameter. Here's what the new code does.

- Adds a string id parameter to the *FAQ* action function

- Creates an *idParameterText* string that we initialise to a default value
- Uses the built-in .Net framework function *string.IsNullOrEmpty* to check if the id parameter contains a value
- If it does we set the *idParameterText* string to a different value, if the id string contains a very specific value (in our case "carrot") then we set the idParameterText string again
- Finally, we output the value of the *idParameterText* string alongside our original content using the Content function

As shown in Figure 2 (below), once our new changes are in place, we should see different responses rendered for each of the following URLs

https://localhost:7262/Help/FAQ
https://localhost: 7262/Help/FAQ/hello
https://localhost: 7262/Help/FAQ/carrot

```
localhost:7262/Help/FAQ
```
Hello! Here is the FAQ. The id parameter was not supplied.

```
localhost:7262/Help/FAQ?id=hello
```
Hello! Here is the FAQ. The id parameter was supplied.

```
localhost:7262/Help/FAQ?id=carrot
```
Hello! Here is the FAQ. The id parameter was supplied, and it's value was carrot.

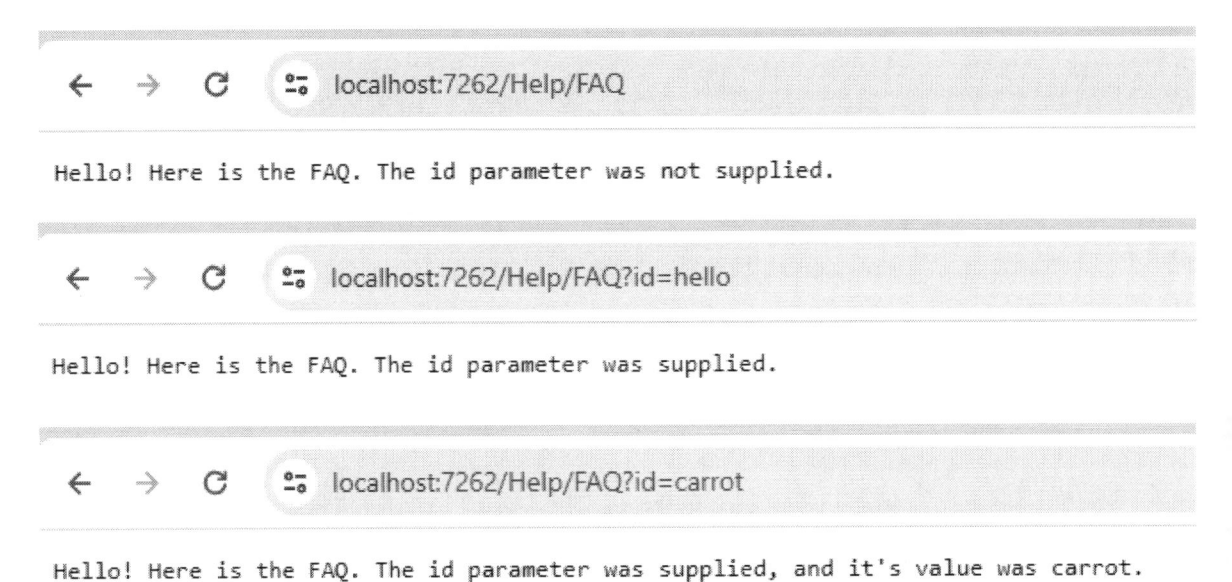

Figure 3 – Different responses for the three different URLs

In addition to the three different URLs listed above the MVC framework will also accept the id parameter as a traditional query string parameter, so the following 3 URLs would also return the same results.

https://localhost:7262/Help/FAQ
https://localhost:7262/Help/FAQ?id=hello
https://localhost:7262/Help/FAQ?id=carrot

At this point, you may wonder why the example doesn't output the value of the id parameter directly into the rendered web page.

The reason for this is that it's bad security practice to include user input in a webpage, and I decided it was best not to do it even in an (admittedly quite contrived) example.

Going into the full details of why you should always sanitize user input is beyond the scope of this chapter, but you can read more about it here https://cheatsheetseries.owasp.org/cheatsheets/Input_Validation_Cheat_Sheet.html

Defining a route that doesn't use the default

So far, we have only looked at routes that used the default route definition, and most of the routes that we'll use in the recipe database app will also use the default route so let's take a moment to define a route that doesn't use the defaults, and an imagine a scenario where we wanted to access our FAQ page via this URL

https://localhost:7262/the-recipe-database-faq-page

To do this we need to define another route in our *program.cs* file, so open the *program.cs* file in Visual Studio Code and add the bold code from the code snippet below (the default rule should already be in your *program.cs* file)

```
app.MapControllerRoute(
    name: "default",
    pattern: "{controller=Home}/{action=Index}/{id?}");


app.MapControllerRoute(
    name: "HelpFAQ",
    pattern: "the-recipe-database-faq-page",
    defaults: new { controller = "Help", action = "FAQ" }
);
```

As you can see from the bold code above, we add a new route with the name "HelpFAQ" and define the pattern argument as the text value (or slug, as it is sometimes called in web terminology) that we're going to use in our URL. We then use the defaults argument, which we have not used before, to tell the MVC framework what controller and action method it should route the request to when it finds our "the-recipe-database-faq-page" pattern.

Now, when we enter the https://localhost:7262/the-recipe-database-faq-page URL into our browser, we should see the FAQ page, as seen in Figure 4.

```
localhost:7262/the-recipe-database-faq-page

Hello! Here is the FAQ. The id parameter was not supplied.
```

Figure 4 – the FAQ page using the non-standard route

In this chapter, we've examined controllers, including how to add a controller and how to return content from it. We've also examined routes, showing how patterns can be used to create routes and how those patterns are used to route requests to specific controller actions. Finally, we've examined how to create custom routes and how to pass parameters via controller actions.

Chapter 5: Working With Views

In the last chapter, we created a controller that wrote content into the response using the *Content* function; in this chapter, we're going to look at the view functionality of the MVC framework to see how we can use it, and the different options it provides us with

By the end of this chapter, you should understand

- How to add a view in your MVC project
- How to call that view from a controller action
- What the Razor view engine does
- How the Razor view engine utilizes the global layout file to render views

Before we start changing any code, we'll add a view file to our project; by default, the first place the MVC Framework looks for a view is this path.

/Views/{ControllerName}/{ActionName}.cshtml

Given this, let's go to Visual Studio Code and add a view in the correct location for our Help controller. Under the *Views* folder, you'll need to add a new folder named *Help* and then under that folder a new file named *FAQ.cshtml*

Figure 1 – our new view file

Once our view has been added, we'll add a bit of dummy content; here's the HTML markup that you should add to the *FAQ.cshtml* file

```
<H2>Hello!</H2>

<p>This is the view!</p>
```

Now we have some markup in place, we can replace the call to the *Content* function with some code that renders the view. Alter the code in the *Controllers/HelpController.cs* file to match this code

```
using Microsoft.AspNetCore.Mvc;

namespace RecipeDatabase.Controllers
{
    public class HelpController : Controller {
        // Action to display a simple message
        public IActionResult FAQ(string id) {

            var idParameterText = " The id parameter was not supplied.";

            if (!string.IsNullOrEmpty(id)) {
                idParameterText = " The id parameter was supplied.";
                if (id == "carrot") {
                    idParameterText = " The id parameter was supplied, and it's value was carrot.";
                }
            }

            return View();
        }
    }
}
```

As you can see from the code, we have just made a one-line change (in bold), but when we visit https://localhost:7262/Help/FAQ we should now see the mark-up from our view

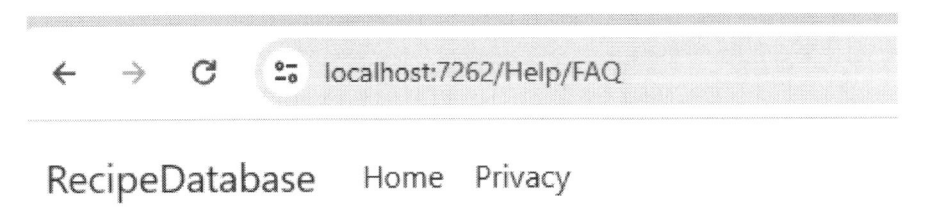

Figure 2 – The view being rendered

As you can see from Figure 2, our HTML markup is now showing in the browser; you may also have noticed a couple of other things.

1. The view completely ignores the code we added in the previous chapter, so we need to fix that.
2. The content is now showing within the site framework; we can see the top menu, etc. So, let's take a look at why that is happening.

The View Engine

When we make the call to the `return View()` function, we pass on the rendering of that page to the ASP.Net MVC engine; by default, the MVC framework uses a view engine named "Razor". In very simple terms this is what the view engine does when we make the *View()* call

1. Locates the corresponding view file based on the view and controller names.
2. Parses the view file. In our current case, there isn't much parsing to be done, but in later examples, the view will need to process data coming from our models.
3. Executes the server-side code within the view file.
4. Generates the final HTML output by combining the static HTML markup and the dynamically generated content.
5. Applies the specified layout (if any) to the generated HTML output.
6. Returns the rendered HTML as the response to the client.

In step 5 of the list above, the framework wraps our view content. By default, the MVC framework uses the file located at *RecipeDatabase\Views\Shared_Layout.cshtml* to render the layout around the view content. Let's take a look at the full markup of that file

```
<!DOCTYPE html>
<html lang="en">
<head>
    <meta charset="utf-8" />
    <meta name="viewport" content="width=device-width, initial-scale=1.0" />
    <title>@ViewData["Title"] - RecipeDatabase</title>
    <link rel="stylesheet" href="~/lib/bootstrap/dist/css/bootstrap.min.css" />
    <link rel="stylesheet" href="~/css/site.css" asp-append-version="true" />
    <link rel="stylesheet" href="~/RecipeDatabase.styles.css" asp-append-version="true" />
</head>
<body>
    <header>
        <nav class="navbar navbar-expand-sm navbar-toggleable-sm navbar-light bg-white border-bottom box-shadow mb-3">
```

```html
            <div class="container-fluid">
                <a class="navbar-brand" asp-area="" asp-controller="Home" asp-action="Index">RecipeDatabase</a>
                <button class="navbar-toggler" type="button" data-bs-toggle="collapse" data-bs-target=".navbar-collapse" aria-controls="navbarSupportedContent"
                        aria-expanded="false" aria-label="Toggle navigation">
                    <span class="navbar-toggler-icon"></span>
                </button>
                <div class="navbar-collapse collapse d-sm-inline-flex justify-content-between">
                    <ul class="navbar-nav flex-grow-1">
                        <li class="nav-item">
                            <a class="nav-link text-dark" asp-area="" asp-controller="Home" asp-action="Index">Home</a>
                        </li>
                        <li class="nav-item">
                            <a class="nav-link text-dark" asp-area="" asp-controller="Home" asp-action="Privacy">Privacy</a>
                        </li>
                    </ul>
                </div>
            </div>
        </nav>
    </header>
    <div class="container">
        <main role="main" class="pb-3">
            @RenderBody()
        </main>
    </div>

    <footer class="border-top footer text-muted">
        <div class="container">
            &copy; 2024 - RecipeDatabase - <a asp-area="" asp-controller="Home" asp-action="Privacy">Privacy</a>
        </div>
    </footer>
    <script src="~/lib/jquery/dist/jquery.min.js"></script>
    <script src="~/lib/bootstrap/dist/js/bootstrap.bundle.min.js"></script>
    <script src="~/js/site.js" asp-append-version="true"></script>
    @await RenderSectionAsync("Scripts", required: false)
</body>
</html>
```

As you can see, there's quite a bit of HTML markup there. If you read through it, you can see the markup that renders the top menu and loads the various scripts the framework uses by default into the page. They include the jQuery JavaScript framework (https://jquery.com/) and the Bootstrap CSS framework (https://getbootstrap.com/). As we have these loaded into the app by default, we will utilize their functionality in later chapters.

You may also notice the bolded call to *@RenderBody()*. The view engine utilizes this call to render the view's contents. After it has located the view file and processed it, the view engine injects the generated content into the layout file at the location where it encounters the *@RenderBody()* call.

Because the view engine works in this way, it is very easy to make site-wide changes to the master layout. Any changes to the *_Layout.cshtml* file will be reflected in any views that use that layout file. For example, if we wanted to change the top menu, we would only have to make that change in the *_Layout.cshtml* file, and then it would be reflected across all views that use that file on the site.

Before we stop discussing the master layout, it would be worth covering how to assign a view to a different layout file. To do this, we'll first create an alternative layout file.

We can do this by creating a file named *_AlternateLayout.cshtml* in the *Views/Shared* folder, once the file has been created enter the code below

```
<!DOCTYPE html>
<html>
<head>
    <title>@ViewBag.Title</title>
    <style>
        body {
            font-family: Arial, sans-serif;
            margin: 0;
            padding: 20px;
        }
        h1 {
            color: #333;
        }
```

```
        .container {
            max-width: 800px;
            margin: 0 auto;
        }
    </style>
</head>
<body>
    <div class="container">
        <h1>My Simple Layout</h1>
        <hr />
        @RenderBody()
        <hr />
        <footer>
            <p>&copy; @DateTime.Now.Year - My Simple Application</p>
        </footer>
    </div>
</body>
</html>
```

Then add the code below to the top of the *Views/FAQ.cshtml* file

```
@{
    Layout = "~/Views/Shared/_AlternateLayout.cshtml";
}
```

Once this is in place, if we navigate to https://localhost:7262/Help/FAQ then we should see the different layout provided by the *_AlternateLayout.cshtml* file.

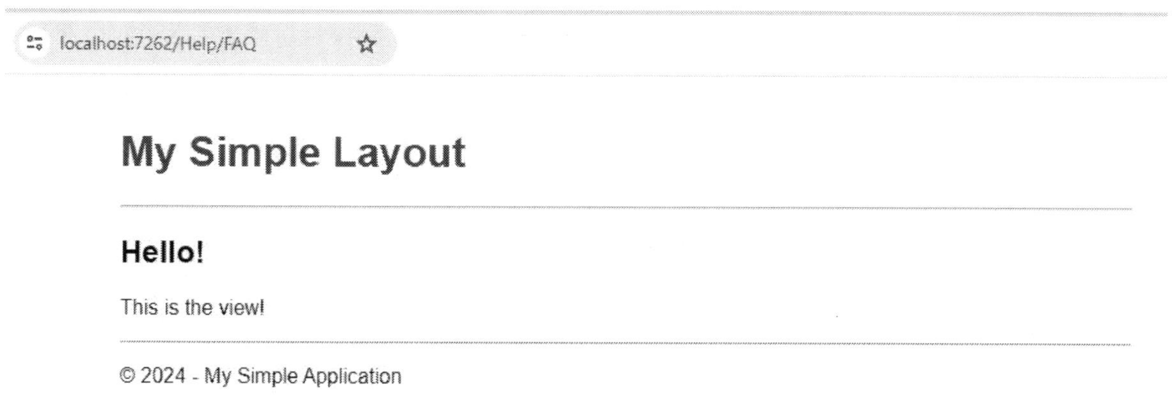
localhost:7262/Help/FAQ
My Simple Layout
Hello!
This is the view!
© 2024 - My Simple Application

Figure 3 – The view rendered in our alternate view

Now we have looked at how the master layout functionality works we can go back to looking at how we can pass data from the controller to the view. Let's remind ourselves of what our *FAQ* method inside our Help controller code looks like

```
public IActionResult FAQ(string id) {

        var idParameterText = " The id parameter was not supplied.";

        if (!string.IsNullOrEmpty(id)) {
                idParameterText = " The id parameter was supplied.";
                if (id == "carrot") {
                        idParameterText = " The id parameter was supplied, and it's value was carrot.";
                }
        }
        return View();
}
```

The controller code above currently contains some logic that calculates a string value based on the id parameter and although this logic is firing we are not doing anything with the result as the call to *return View();* does not pass any information on to the view, and we currently have no logic in our view to display information passed from the controller.

So let's make a very simple change to pass the idParameterText value to our view, change the code in the *Controllers/HelpController.cs* file to this code

```
public IActionResult FAQ(string id) {

    var idParameterText = " The id parameter was not supplied.";

    if (!string.IsNullOrEmpty(id)) {
            idParameterText = " The id parameter was supplied.";
            if (id == "carrot") {
                    idParameterText = " The id parameter was supplied, and it's value was carrot.";
            }
    }

    ViewData["ParameterText"] = idParameterText;

    return View();
}
```

As you can see from the bolded code, we have added one line

ViewData["ParameterText"] = idParameterText;

This line takes the value of the *idParametetText* variable and assigns it to the *ViewData* dictionary with the key *"ParameterText"*.

The *ViewData* dictionary is a feature provided by ASP.NET MVC that allows data to be passed from the controller to the view. It acts like a container or bag where you can store data that you want to make available to the view during the rendering process. In our example, the *ViewData* dictionary is being used to store a piece of data under the key "*ParameterText."*

This key is paired with the value contained in the variable *idParameterText*. Essentially, whatever value is held by the *idParameterText* variable at the time this line of code is executed is placed into the *ViewData* dictionary under the name "*ParameterText*". When the view is rendered, this value can be retrieved using the same key, enabling dynamic content to be displayed based on the value passed from the controller.

Using *ViewData* is particularly handy when you have small amounts of data to pass between the controller and the view without needing a strongly typed view model. It's flexible and straightforward to use, though it does require you to remember the type of data you've stored and to cast it appropriately when retrieving it in the view.

Now let's take a look at the changes we need to make to our view code in the *Views/Help/FAQ.cshtml* file

```
@{
Layout = "~/Views/Shared/_AlternateLayout.cshtml";
}

<H2>Hello!</H2>

<p>This is the view! @ViewData["ParameterText"]</p>
```

As you can see from the bolded code we have made a small change that retrieves the "*ParameterText*" value from the ViewData dictionary that we populated in the controller. We add an @ symbol before *ViewData["ParameterText"]* to tell the Razor view engine that it needs to process this as code to retrieve the *ViewData* value rather than just rendering HTML markup. We will continue to use the @ symbol in later code examples to render things like if statements and loops in our view code.

ViewBag vs ViewData

To pass the data in our example, we used the *ViewData* dictionary, but there is another way we could have passed the data: using the *ViewBag* object. To conclude this chapter, we'll examine the two methods and discuss their strengths and weaknesses.

In ASP.NET MVC, both *ViewData* and *ViewBag* are used to pass data from the controller to the view. They help make data available during a page's rendering without requiring a strongly typed view model.

ViewData Example

```
<h2>ViewData Example</h2>

<p>The count is: @(ViewData["Count"] != null ? ViewData["Count"].ToString() : "")</p>


@if ((int)ViewData["Count"] > 3)

{
    <p>The count is greater than 3.</p>

}
```

The *ViewData* dictionary is a dynamic container which means you can store any type of data in it. In the example above, *ViewData* is used to store and display a count. The Razor syntax checks if the *Count* key exists and is not null, converting it to a string for display.

After we've output the value, we need to do an integer comparison using *ViewData["Count"]*; as the dictionary value will be an object, we need to convert it to an integer to get the if statement to work as expected. This demonstrates how *ViewData* requires casting and checking for null values to avoid runtime errors, which can be a bit cumbersome.

View Bag Example

```
<h2>ViewBag Example</h2>

<p>The count is: @ViewBag.Count</p>


@if (ViewBag.Count > 3)
{
    <p>The count is greater than 3.</p>
}
```

ViewBag offers a more dynamic approach to passing data to the view. It is essentially a wrapper around *ViewData*, providing a dynamic object that allows you to add or access properties more naturally. In the *ViewBag* example, the count is accessed directly without the need for casting or calling methods like *ToString()*. The syntax used with *ViewBag* is cleaner and more straightforward. However, like ViewData, it lacks compile-time type checking, which can lead to errors that only appear at runtime if you are not careful.

To expand on this, a bit more, the view code in the last example will only work if we set *ViewBag.Count* to an integer value in our controller

```
ViewBag.Count = 3
```

If we set it to a string value

```
ViewBag.Count = "3"
```

Then the code will compile successfully but when we access the view in a browser it will throw an error

> localhost:7262/Help/FAQ
>
> **An unhandled exception occurred while processing the request.**
>
> RuntimeBinderException: Operator '>' cannot be applied to operands of type 'string' and 'int'
>
> CallSite.Target(Closure , CallSite , object , int)
>
> **Stack**   Query   Cookies   Headers   Routing
>
> **RuntimeBinderException: Operator '>' cannot be applied to operands of type 'string' and 'int'**
>
> CallSite.Target(Closure , CallSite , object , int)
> System.Dynamic.UpdateDelegates.UpdateAndExecute2<T0, T1, TRet>(CallSite site, T0 arg0, T1 arg1)
> AspNetCoreGeneratedDocument.Views_Help_FAQ.ExecuteAsync() in **FAQ.cshtml**
> | 12. @if (ViewBag.Count > 3)
> Microsoft.AspNetCore.Mvc.Razor.RazorView.RenderPageCoreAsync(IRazorPage page, ViewContext context)

Figure 4 – a run time caused by trying to use a string value as an integer

Ultimately, both *ViewBag* and *ViewData* serve the same purpose but differ in their ease of use and method of access. Choosing between them often comes down to personal preference or specific scenarios where one might slightly edge out the other in terms of readability or convenience. Whilst both methods are quick and convenient, the danger of errors like the one in Figure 3 is one of the reasons why people tend to prefer using strongly typed models to pass data between the controller and the view. We'll take a closer look at how to pass data using a model in our next chapter.

Chapter 6: Working With Models

In the last chapter, we looked at passing information from the controller to the view using the *ViewData* and *ViewBag* functionality. However, the MVC framework lends itself to passing information around using models. In this chapter, we'll look at how to code a very simple model, populate it in our controller, and show how we can use the view engine to output our model data.

Firstly, let's create the model code; in the *Models* folder of your project, create a file named *Recipe.cs* and paste the code below into it

```
namespace RecipeDatabase.Models
{
    public class Recipe
    {
        public int Id { get; set; }
        public string Name { get; set; }
        public string Category { get; set; }
        public string? ImagePath { get; set; }
        public string Description { get; set; }
        public string RecipeInstructions { get; set; }
    }
}
```

Code Explanation

There isn't much to say about the model code; we have just defined a simple class that holds the properties corresponding to the information that we need to hold in our Recipe objects.

Before looking at the controller code, we'll need to create a Recipe controller, so let's add a new file to the *Controllers* folder with the name *RecipeController.cs*

Once the file has been created, copy the following code into it.

```csharp
using Microsoft.AspNetCore.Mvc;
using RecipeDatabase.Models;

namespace RecipeDatabase.Controllers
{
    public class RecipeController : Controller
    {
        public IActionResult Recipe()
        {

            var recipe = new Recipe();
            recipe.Name = "Cheese Toastie";
            recipe.Category = "Snacks";
            recipe.Description = "A luxurious sandwich fit for any meal";
            recipe.ImagePath = @"\images\cheesetoastie.webp";
            recipe.RecipeInstructions = "1. Preheat a skillet or griddle over medium heat.<br>2. Butter one side of each bread slice.<br>3. Place one slice of bread, butter side down, on the skillet.<br>4. Add the cheese slices on top of the bread in the skillet, covering the entire surface.<br>5. Place the second slice of bread on top of the cheese, butter side up.<br>6. Cook for 2-3 minutes, or until the bottom slice is golden brown and the cheese starts to melt.<br>7. Carefully flip the sandwich using a spatula and cook the other side for an additional 2-3 minutes, or until golden brown and the cheese is fully melted.<br>8. Remove the cheese toastie from the skillet and let it cool for a minute.<br>9. Cut the sandwich diagonally into two triangles.<br>10. Serve hot and enjoy your delicious cheese toastie!";

            return View(recipe);
        }

    }
}
```

Code Explanation

The controller code is also reasonably straightforward we begin by creating a new recipe object

```
var recipe = new Recipe();
```

Then on the next few lines we populate the model properties, and finally we pass the populated *recipe* object to the view

```
return View(recipe);
```

Here, we only need to pass the recipe object as an argument to the View function. Our view will share the same name as the controller action function, so the framework will automatically use the correct view file.

If we had wanted to use a view file with a different name to the controller action then we would have needed to have specified it in the call to the *View* function

```
return View("Recipe", recipe);
```

To create our view we'll create a folder named *Recipe* in the *Views* folder, we'll then create a view file named *Recipe.cshtml* in that folder

Here's the view code that we will add to the file

```
@model RecipeDatabase.Models.Recipe

@{
    ViewBag.Title = Model.Name;
}


<div class="container">
    <div class="row">
        <div class="col-md-6">
            <img src="@Model.ImagePath" alt="@Model.Name" class="img-fluid">
        </div>
        <div class="col-md-6">
            <h1>@Model.Name</h1>
            <h4>Category: @Model.Category</h4>
            <hr>
            <h3>Description:</h3>
            <p>@Html.Raw(Model.Description)</p>
            <h3>Instructions:</h3>

            <p>@Html.Raw(Model.RecipeInstructions.Replace("\n","<br>"))</p>

        </div>
    </div>
</div>
```

Code Explanation

At the top of the view file in MVC, you'll notice a model declaration.

`@model RecipeDatabase.Models.Recipe`

This declaration is crucial because it binds a specific model, in this case, our Recipe model directly to the view. This setup not only provides direct access to the properties of the model within the view but also allows you to pass an instance of the model from the MVC controller to the view. This is particularly useful when dealing with forms, which we'll explore in later chapters as we delve into creating, editing, and deleting recipes.

Once we have defined the model at the top of a view, we can access the model using the *@Model* syntax. You can see a number of places in the code, where we are using *@Model* to output the model's data, for example, the lines below

`<h1>@Model.Name</h1>`

`<h4>Category: @Model.Category</h4>`

Write out the model's name and category properties in the view file.

Now that we have a controller and a view named *Recipe* we should be able to access the view using this URL

https://localhost:7262/Recipe/Recipe

If you input the URL into your browser (remembering to change the port number) you should see something similar to Figure 1

Figure 1 - Recipe data displayed inside the recipe view

What does @Html.Raw do?

You might have noticed in the code that we use the *@Html.Raw* helper method to output the *Description* and *RecipeInstruction* properties from the model.

```
<p>@Html.Raw(Model.RecipeInstructions)</p>
```

@Html.Raw is a helper method used in ASP.NET MVC to output HTML content exactly as it's written, without encoding it. Normally, when you output content using standard Razor syntax like *@Model.Name*, the content is encoded to prevent security issues like cross-site scripting (XSS), where harmful scripts could be injected into the page. This encoding turns special HTML characters like < and > into their safe representations, which stops any HTML or scripts from being rendered as code.

However, when you use *@Html.Raw*, it tells the Razor view engine to output the string exactly as it is, including any HTML tags or JavaScript code it might contain. This can be useful when you want to display HTML elements that are dynamically generated or stored in a database, such as formatted text or a dynamic user interface component. However, it should be used carefully, as it can open security risks if the content isn't properly sanitized beforehand.

In the case of our recipe app, we may need to use HTML tags such as paragraphs or lists to lay out the description or recipe instructions, so we allow these fields to be output as HTML. If you were going to write an app where you thought security could be an issue, then you need to give further consideration to where you allowed *@Html.Raw to be used.*

A note about images

As you can see from Figure 1, the recipe database shows images along with the recipes. If you're coding along with the examples in the book, you won't have access to the images, so what you see in your browser will look slightly different.

If you'd like the images, please drop an email to ian@hardworkingnerd.com, and I'll send you all the code that is used in the book. The code will include all the images you need to set up the recipe database.

CHAPTER 7: CONNECTING UP TO A DATABASE

In the last chapter, we looked at using a very simple model where the values were hard coded.

We now need to integrate our model with a database, which will allow us to easily add, edit, and delete recipe/model data.

For this project, we are choosing SQLite as our database because:

- It is extremely lightweight; the entire database is contained within a single file.
- It is easy and quick to install across multiple platforms.
- The website can be deployed straightforwardly since the database only requires a single file.
- As the database is file-based, there are no additional hosting charges when we deploy the application.

While SQLite is an excellent choice for small projects, if you are planning to deploy a solution with hundreds or thousands of concurrent users, you might find a different database solution better suited to your needs.

You can run SQLite queries from the command line. To get started:

1. Download the command line tools from **https://sqlite.org/download.html**. Make sure to download the appropriate version for the operating system you are using. As shown in Figure 1

Precompiled Binaries for Windows

sqlite-dll-win-x86-3450300.zip (1.01 MiB)	32-bit DLL (x86) for SQLite version 3.45.3. (SHA3-256: b5d01cccf1cea00b4250bc26d3941ba29b16eaaaa7ce9fe9f7776b8e4491ff2f)
sqlite-dll-win-x64-3450300.zip (1.26 MiB)	64-bit DLL (x64) for SQLite version 3.45.3. (SHA3-256: 9631cadef7d48498a468be6dd0dba825af3121f0980109601168f695f4273688)
sqlite-tools-win-x64-3450300.zip (4.77 MiB)	A bundle of command-line tools for managing SQLite database files, including the command-line shell program, the sqldiff.exe program, and the sqlite3_analyzer.exe program. 64-bit. (SHA3-256: 429cca813471884ff3c9b51697ecc1e6750fb947ab5cd91efb098c6fbc1f4053)

Figure 1 – the download you'll need if you're working on a Windows machine

2. Extract the tools from the zip file to a directory named 'sqlite'.
3. Open a command line in the sqlite directory

4. To create a blank database file, use the command: **sqlite3 recipedatabase.db "VACUUM;"**

Once you have run the command in the final step, you should see a recipedatabase.db file has been created inside your sqlite directory, as shown in Figure 2

Name	Date modified	Type	Size
recipedatabase.db	24/04/2024 06:05	Data Base File	4 KB
sqldiff.exe	24/04/2024 06:04	Application	3,025 KB
sqlite3.exe	24/04/2024 06:04	Application	3,647 KB
sqlite3_analyzer.exe	24/04/2024 06:04	Application	4,266 KB

Figure 2 – the *recipedatabse.db* file

Leave the file where it is for now; we will come back to it later in the chapter.

As well as using SQLite, we are also going to utilize Entity Framework functionality that will create and populate database tables for us based on our Recipe model. To add this functionality to our project, we need to run the commands below via the terminal in Visual Studio Code.

```
dotnet tool install --global dotnet-ef
dotnet add package Microsoft.EntityFrameworkCore.Sqlite
dotnet add package Microsoft.EntityFrameworkCore.Design
```

Make sure you are inside the recipe database folder before running the commands. If you get an error like *"Could not find any project in ..."* then run

```
cd recipedatabase
```

and try the commands again.

Now that we have created our SQLite database and added the Entity Framework packages for our project, we need to add some code to allow the Entity Framework to connect to our database, so we can query it when we start building our sample application.

Before we start adding the code that will hook up our MVC application to our database, we will need to define the model that we want our database table to be based on. To do this, we can use the model that we created in the previous chapter, which should be in a file named *Recipe.cs* in the *Models* folder of your project. Here's a reminder of what the code looked like

```
namespace RecipeDatabase.Models
{
    public class Recipe
    {
        public int Id { get; set; }
        public string Name { get; set; }
        public string Category { get; set; }
        public string? ImagePath { get; set; }
        public string Description { get; set; }
        public string RecipeInstructions { get; set; }
    }
}
```

Now, we are going to add some classes to help the Entity Framework link our model to our SQLite database.

To do this we'll add a Folder named Data to our project

Figure 3 - The Data folder

We will then add a file named *ApplicationDbContext.cs* to the folder. Once the file has been added, add the following code

```csharp
using Microsoft.EntityFrameworkCore;
using RecipeDatabase.Models;

namespace RecipeDatabase.Data
{
    public class ApplicationDbContext : DbContext
    {
        public ApplicationDbContext(DbContextOptions<ApplicationDbContext> options)
            : base(options)
        {
        }

        public DbSet<Recipe> Recipes { get; set; }
    }
}
```

Code Explanation

Most of the code in the *ApplicationDbContext.cs* is boilerplate code required by the Entity Framework, but this line

```csharp
public DbSet<Recipe> Recipes { get; set; }
```

is what informs the Entity Framework that we want it to build a Recipes table in our database and generate the code to query the database table and write, edit, and delete the records in it.

Once the Entity Framework has created the table, it will contain no data, so we'll also add a class to seed our Recipe table with some sample data.

To do this, we'll create a file in the *Data* folder named *DbInitializer.cs* and then add the following code

```csharp
using Microsoft.EntityFrameworkCore;
using RecipeDatabase.Models;

namespace RecipeDatabase.Data
{
    public static class DbInitializer
    {
        public static void Initialize(IServiceProvider serviceProvider)
        {
            using (var context = new ApplicationDbContext(
                serviceProvider.GetRequiredService<DbContextOptions<ApplicationDbContext>>()))
            {
                // Look for any recipes. If there are any, the DB has been seeded
                if (context.Recipes.Any())
                {
                    return; // DB has been seeded
                }

                context.Recipes.AddRange(
                    new Recipe { Name = "Burgers", Category = "Main Courses", ImagePath=@"\images\burgers.jpg", Description = "Classic beef burgers topped with fresh lettuce, ripe tomatoes, and gooey cheese. Perfect for a casual dinner or a backyard barbecue.", RecipeInstructions = "1. Grill beef patties until cooked to desired doneness.<br>2. Toast buns on the grill for a minute.<br>3. Add lettuce, tomato, cheese, and patties to buns.<br>4. Serve with ketchup, mustard, or your favorite burger sauce.<br>" },

                    new Recipe { Name = "Pizza", Category = "Main Courses", ImagePath=@"\images\pizza.jpg", Description = "Homemade pizza layered with savory tomato sauce, mozzarella cheese, and a selection of toppings to fit any taste. Ideal for family movie nights.", RecipeInstructions = "1. Spread sauce on rolled out dough.<br>2. Sprinkle cheese generously.<br>3. Add toppings of your choice.<br>4. Bake in preheated oven at 475°F for 12-15 minutes.<br>" },
```

```
                    new Recipe { Name = "Spaghetti Bolognese", Category = "Main
Courses", ImagePath=@"\images\spaghetti_bolognese.jpg", Description = "A hearty
Italian dish featuring spaghetti topped with a meaty tomato sauce. A comfort food
favorite that's both satisfying and delicious.", RecipeInstructions = "1. Cook
spaghetti according to package instructions.<br>2. Brown meat in a pan, add
tomato sauce, and simmer.<br>3. Serve hot sauce over drained spaghetti.<br>" }
                    );

                    context.SaveChanges();
                }
            }
        }
}
```

Code Explanation

In the class, we have a single function named Initialize

```
public static void Initialize(IServiceProvider serviceProvider)
        {
            using (var context = new ApplicationDbContext(
serviceProvider.GetRequiredService<DbContextOptions<ApplicationDbContext>>()))
                {
```

We pass in an *IServiceProvider* object named *serviceProvider*, and the function uses it to create a context object; the *context* object is then used to add the data to the database.

The code used to create the context is similar to the Inversion of Control functionality that we'll look at later in the book. For the purposes of our database app, you don't really need to understand how all this fits together, so for now; we'll just leave it that an object is created that allows us to check for and add objects to the database.

Once the context object has been created, we use it to check to see if there are any records already in the database

```
if (context.Recipes.Any())
{
        return; // DB has been seeded
}
```

If we find any records in the database then we return from the function, so the seed code will only run on an empty database.

If there are no records in the database then we add some Recipe models to the Recipe collection on the context object

```
context.Recipes.AddRange(
                new Recipe { Name = "Burgers",
                //code continues to add object data
        );
```

Then, use the context object again to save the *Recipe* objects into the database.

```
Context.SaveChanges();
```

Altering the program.cs file

Now we have the setup code in place we need to add some code to the program.cs file to hook everything up; in the code below, I've included the entire text of the program.cs file and formatted the added lines in bold

```csharp
using Microsoft.EntityFrameworkCore;
using RecipeDatabase.Data;


var builder = WebApplication.CreateBuilder(args);
// Add services to the container.
Builder.Services.AddControllersWithViews();
builder.Services.AddDbContext<ApplicationDbContext>(options =>
    options.UseSqlite(builder.Configuration.GetConnectionString("DefaultConnection"))
);
var app = builder.Build();
// Configure the HTTP request pipeline.
If (!app.Environment.IsDevelopment())
{
    app.UseExceptionHandler("/Home/Error");
    // The default HSTS value is 30 days. You may want to change this for production scenarios, see https://aka.ms/aspnetcore-hsts.
    App.UseHsts();
}


using (var scope = app.Services.CreateScope())
{
    var services = scope.ServiceProvider;

    var context = services.GetRequiredService<ApplicationDbContext>();
    context.Database.Migrate(); // Ensure the database is created and migrated
    DbInitializer.Initialize(services); // Seed the database
}

app.UseHttpsRedirection();
app.UseStaticFiles();
```

```
app.UseRouting();

app.UseAuthorization();

app.MapControllerRoute(
    name: "default",
    pattern: "{controller=Home}/{action=Index}/{id?}");

app.MapControllerRoute(
    name: "HelpFAQ",
    pattern: "the-recipe-database-faq-page",
    defaults: new { controller = "Help", action = "FAQ" }
);
app.Run();
```

Code Explanation

We add a line at the top of the file to include the required entity framework functionality

```
using Microsoft.EntityFrameworkCore;
```

A line is then added to hook up our *ApplicationDbContext* class so it can be injected into our controller classes (we'll go into greater depth about this in the next chapter). We also pass the connection string for our SQLite database into this code. We'll add the connection string to the *appsetting.json* file in our project shortly.

```
builder.Services.AddDbContext<ApplicationDbContext>(options =>
options.UseSqlite(builder.Configuration.GetConnectionString("DefaultConnection"))
);
```

Once the configuration is complete, it's important to ensure that the database is ready for use. This involves applying any pending migrations to update or create the database schema and optionally seeding the database with initial data:

```
using (var scope = app.Services.CreateScope())
{
    var services = scope.ServiceProvider;

    var context = services.GetRequiredService<ApplicationDbContext>();
    context.Database.Migrate(); // Ensure the database is created and migrated
    DbInitializer.Initialize(services); // Seed the database
}
```

This step is essential to make sure the database structure is up-to-date and ready. Seeding the database can be very useful, especially in development environments, but should be handled with caution in production environments.

All the code should now be in place for the database, but we need to make sure that the database file is where we need it to be, to do this, we'll create a folder in our project named *Database*

We'll then copy the *recipedatabase.db* file that we created earlier in this chapter to the Database directory.

Figure 4 - The Database folder with the *recipedatabase.db* file inside it

Finally, we need to update the *appsetting.json* file in our project to point at our database file

```
{
  "ConnectionStrings": {
    "DefaultConnection": "Data Source=Database/recipedatabase.db"
  },
  "Logging": {
    "LogLevel": {
      "Default": "Information",
      "Microsoft.AspNetCore": "Warning"
    }
  },
  "AllowedHosts": "*"
}
```

Again, I have included the entire contents of the *appsetting.json* file above and bolded the section that needs to be added.

Running the Entity Framework Migrations

Now we have the necessary code in place we can run the Entity Framework functionality to create our migrations, we can do this by running the following commands from the Terminal inside Visual Studio Code

```
dotnet ef migrations add InitialCreate
```

```
dotnet ef database update
```

After running these two commands, the Recipe database table should be created, but the initial data won't be added to the table until the seed code in the **Program.cs** file is executed. To run this code, start the project from the debug section of Visual Studio Code.

That should have set up our database and seeded the sample data. To check this open a command prompt from the Database folder inside the MVC project (you can do this on Windows by navigating to the folder in Windows Explorer and then typing *cmd* into the address bar) once you have opened the cmd prompt type

```
C:\sqlite\sqlite3 recipedatabase.db
```

You will need to change this command slightly if you did not install the SQLite client tools in the C:\sqlite directory, after issuing the command you should see the SQLite command prompt displayed

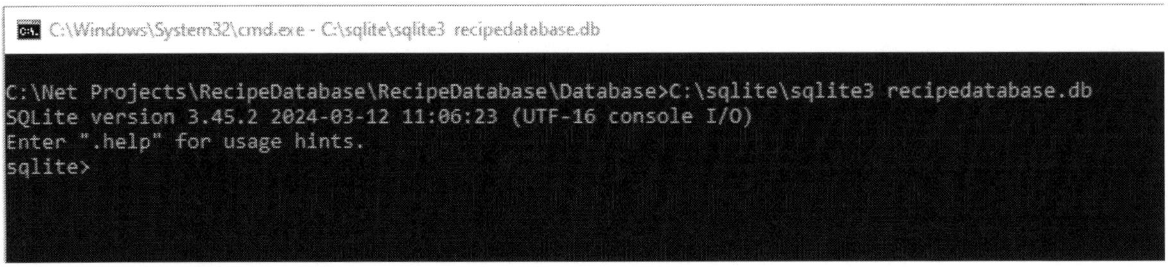
C:\Windows\System32\cmd.exe - C:\sqlite\sqlite3 recipedatabase.db
C:\Net Projects\RecipeDatabase\RecipeDatabase\Database>C:\sqlite\sqlite3 recipedatabase.db
SQLite version 3.45.2 2024-03-12 11:06:23 (UTF-16 console I/O)
Enter ".help" for usage hints.
sqlite>

Figure 5 - The SQLite prompt in a command window

We can now issue the *.tables* command to list the tables in our *recipedatabase.db* database, so type

```
.tables
```

into the command prompt

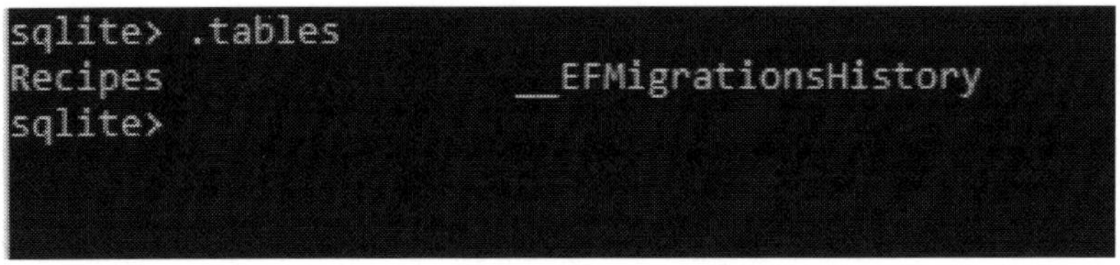
sqlite> .tables
Recipes __EFMigrationsHistory
sqlite>

Figure 5 - The tables in our database listed after we have run the *.tables* command

As you can see from Figure 5, the database contains two tables, *Recipes* and *__EFMigrationHistory*. The *__EFMigrationHistory* table is a table that the Entity framework creates to keep track of our migrations, so we don't need to worry about that. The *Recipes* table should contain all of our recipe data, and it's the table we will use to build our app, we can check there is data in the table by issuing a select statement from the command window

```
Select * from recipes;
```

```
C:\Net Projects\RecipeDatabase\RecipeDatabase\Database>C:\sqlite\sqlite3 recipedatabase.db
SQLite version 3.45.2 2024-03-12 11:06:23 (UTF-16 console I/O)
Enter ".help" for usage hints.
sqlite> select * from recipes;
1|Main Courses|Classic beef burgers topped with fresh lettuce, ripe tomatoes, and gooey cheese. Perfect fo
r a casual dinner or a backyard barbecue.|\images\burgers.jpg|Burgers|1. Grill beef patties until cooked t
o desired doneness.<br>2. Toast buns on the grill for a minute.<br>3. Add lettuce, tomato, cheese, and pat
ties to buns.<br>4. Serve with ketchup, mustard, or your favorite burger sauce.<br>
2|Main Courses|Homemade pizza layered with savory tomato sauce, mozzarella cheese, and a selection of topp
ings to fit any taste. Ideal for family movie nights.|\images\pizza.jpg|Pizza|1. Spread sauce on rolled ou
t dough.<br>2. Sprinkle cheese generously.<br>3. Add toppings of your choice.<br>4. Bake in preheated oven
 at 475°F for 12-15 minutes.<br>
3|Main Courses|A hearty Italian dish featuring spaghetti topped with a meaty tomato sauce. A comfort food
favorite that's both satisfying and delicious.|\images\spaghetti_bolognese.jpg|Spaghetti Bolognese|1. Cook
 spaghetti according to package instructions.<br>2. Brown meat in a pan, add tomato sauce, and simmer.<br>
3. Serve hot sauce over drained spaghetti.<br>
4|Main Courses|Layers of pasta, rich meat sauce, and creamy ricotta cheese, baked to perfection. A great m
eal to feed a crowd or enjoy leftovers the next day.|\images\lasagna.jpg|Lasagna|1. Prepare meat sauce and
 ricotta mixture.<br>2. Layer lasagna sheets with cheese and sauce in a baking dish.<br>3. Bake covered at
 375°F for 45 minutes, then uncover and bake for an additional 15 minutes.<br>
5|Main Courses|A creamy, cheesy macaroni dish that's a favorite among kids and adults alike. Easy to make
and endlessly customizable with your favorite cheeses.|\images\macaroni_cheese.jpg|Macaroni Cheese|1. Boil
 macaroni until al dente.<br>2. Prepare a cheese sauce with butter, flour, milk, and cheese.<br>3. Combine
 macaroni and sauce, top with breadcrumbs.<br>4. Bake until bubbly and golden on top.<br>
6|Breakfast|Light and fluffy pancakes served with warm maple syrup and fresh berries. A delightful way to
```

Figure 5 - The tables in our database listed after we have run the *.tables* command

As you can see from Figure 5, although it's not presented in the most visually pleasing way, we can see our data has been added to the recipes table.

As a recap, here's what has happened to get data into our database

- The entity framework has created a recipes table in the SQLite database that we created
- The code in the *DbInitializer.cs* file in the *Data* folder has run and added records into the database

There's obviously quite a lot going on here, but in order to keep this book reasonably brief, I'm not going to explain everything that the Entity Framework is doing behind the scenes. We will just accept that the database tables have been created based on our model code and then move on to the next steps of creating our recipe database app.

Entity Framework Scaffolding

It is possible to get the Entity Framework to write controllers and views that will handle all

the create, edit, and delete functionality for us. However, this functionality is currently only available if you use an SQL server to host your database, as explained here: https://github.com/dotnet/Scaffolding/issues/1653.

This is definitely worth considering if you're embarking on a project that will require a lot of models and CRUD (create, read, update, and delete) functionality. However, for our purposes, it will be beneficial to go through and understand how we create the add, edit, and delete code, so we are going to write the code ourselves.

Summary

Now that we have a database layer in place and some seed data, we can begin to use that in our recipe application. In the next chapter, we'll start looking at how to query the database and use it to create functionality to list all of the recipe details in the database and display recipe details from the database.

Remember that if you'd like all the code used in this book, including all the recipe data that I've slightly truncated in the chapter, please email ian@hardworkingnerd.com, and I'll send you everything you need. I'll also include all the images you need to set up the recipe database and a ready-built SQLite database containing all the required data.

Chapter 8: Retrieving a recipe from the database and viewing it

In this chapter, we're going to do two things

1. Create some functionality that lists all the recipes in the database, so the user can choose which recipe they would like to see the details of. As this could get difficult to navigate quite quickly, we will extend it by adding search functionality in the next chapter.
2. Modify the Recipe controller and view we implemented in the last chapter so that they return data from the database instead of hard-coded dummy data.

We'll use the recipe controller for the list screen we just need to add a new action method to the *RecipeController.cs* file in the *Controllers* folder

```
public IActionResult Recipes()
{
    var recipes = from r in _context.Recipes
                  select r;

    return View(recipes);
}
```

The code snippet above shows that we are using a _context object to access the database. This object is an instance of the *ApplicationDbContext* class, which we introduced in Chapter 7. The MVC framework delivers this object to our controller through a mechanism called Inversion of Control (IoC). Essentially, IoC allows the framework to manage the creation and delivery of dependencies like our database context.

This method greatly simplifies managing dependencies ourselves, promoting a more modular and maintainable code structure.

Below is the code snippet showing how the *_context* object is integrated into our *RecipeController*

```
public class RecipeController : Controller {

        private readonly ApplicationDbContext _context;

        public RecipeController(ApplicationDbContext context)
        {
            _context = context;
        }
```

This pattern, where the MVC framework supplies the required *ApplicationDbContext* to the *RecipeController*, is a good example of IoC. By receiving dependencies via the constructor, the controller becomes easier to test and maintain because it doesn't have to concern itself with the complexities of creating and managing the lifecycle of the underlying database connection.

In very simple terms here's the process that gets the context object into our controller

1. **Entering the URL**: When you type a URL into your browser, you're asking for a specific page or action.
2. **Finding the Right Controller**: The MVC system looks at the URL and decides which controller should handle your request.
3. **Setting Up the Controller**: Before the MVC system creates the controller, it checks if the controller needs any tools or information to do its job, like accessing the database.
4. **Giving What's Needed**: If the controller needs something specific, like a way to talk to the database, the MVC system provides it automatically when the controller is created. Thus, the controller is ready to go as soon as you need it.

This process makes sure that whenever a controller starts up, it has everything it needs right away, making it ready to handle the request effectively.

All of the plumbing code provided by the Entity Framework means that we can access a collection of all the recipes in the database using a small amount of code

```
var recipes = from r in _context.Recipes
              select r;
```

We can then pass the collection on to the view.

Because we've changed quite a lot of the controller code, let's reprint the entire *RecipeController.cs* file so if you're coding along, you can be sure you've got everything you need

```csharp
using Microsoft.AspNetCore.Mvc;
using RecipeDatabase.Data;
using RecipeDatabase.Models;

namespace RecipeDatabase.Controllers
{
    public class RecipeController : Controller
    {
        private readonly ApplicationDbContext _context;

        public RecipeController(ApplicationDbContext context)
        {
            _context = context;
        }

        public  IActionResult Recipes()
        {

            var recipes = from r in _context.Recipes
                        select r;

            return View(recipes);
        }

        public IActionResult Recipe()
        {

            var recipe = new Recipe();
            recipe.Name = "Cheese Toastie";
            recipe.Category = "Snacks";
            recipe.Description = "A luxurious sandwich fit for any meal";
            recipe.ImagePath = @"\images\cheesetoastie.webp";
            recipe.RecipeInstructions = "1. Preheat a skillet or griddle over medium heat.<br>2. Butter one side of each bread slice.<br>3. Place one slice of bread, butter side down, on the skillet.<br>4. Add the cheese slices on top of the bread in the skillet, covering the entire surface.<br>5. Place the second slice of bread on top of the cheese, butter side up.<br>6. Cook for 2-3 minutes, or until the bottom slice is golden brown and the cheese starts to melt.<br>7. Carefully flip the sandwich using a spatula and cook the other side for an additional 2-3 minutes, or until golden brown and the cheese is fully melted.<br>8. Remove the cheese toastie from the skillet and let it cool for a minute.<br>9. Cut the sandwich diagonally into two triangles.<br>10. Serve hot and enjoy your delicious cheese toastie!";

            return View(recipe);
        }

    }
```

}

Now let's take a look at creating the view code, create a file named *Recipes.cshtml* in the *Views/Recipe* directory and add the code below to it

```
@model IQueryable<Recipe>

@{
    ViewBag.Title = "Recipes";
}

<div class="container my-4">
    <h1 class="mb-3">Recipes</h1>

    <!-- Recipes List -->
    <div class="row">
        @foreach (var recipe in Model)
        {
            <div class="col-md-4 mb-4">
                <div class="card h-100">
                    <img class="card-img-top" src="@recipe.ImagePath" alt="@recipe.Name">
                    <div class="card-body d-flex flex-column">
                        <h5 class="card-title">@recipe.Name</h5>
                        <p class="card-text">@recipe.Description</p>
                        <a href="@Url.Action("Recipe", "Recipe", new { id = recipe.Id })" class="btn btn-primary mt-auto">View Recipe</a>
                    </div>
                </div>
            </div>
        }
    </div>
</div>
```

Code Explanation

We passed the results of a LINQ query that used the *_context* object to the View in the controller

```
var recipes = from r in _context.Recipes
              select r;

return View(recipes);
```

so we need to define a Model that matches what we have passed. Here's what we use

```
@model IQueryable<Recipe>
```

After that, we add a for each loop using Razor syntax that loops through each item in the recipe collection

```
@foreach (var recipe in Model)
        {
            <div class="col-md-4 mb-4">
                <div class="card h-100">
                    <img class="card-img-top" src="@recipe.ImagePath" alt="@recipe.Name">
                        <div class="card-body d-flex flex-column">
                            <h5 class="card-title">@recipe.Name</h5>
                            <p class="card-text">@recipe.Description</p>
                            <a href="@Url.Action("Recipe", "Recipe", new { id = recipe.Id })" class="btn btn-primary mt-auto">View Recipe</a>
                        </div>
                </div>
            </div>
        }
```

The loop outputs details of each recipe into some HTML markup; it also uses the *URL.Action* method to create a link to each recipe so we can drill down into each of the recipe details

```
<a href="@Url.Action("Recipe", "Recipe", new { id = recipe.Id })" class="btn btn-primary mt-auto">View Recipe</a>
```

We pass the action method name and the controller name to *URL.Action* function along with the id parameter of the recipe, the function then constructs a link URL for us, here's a sample URL for one of the recipes

https://localhost:7262/Recipe/Recipe/2

After all the controller and view code has been added you can see what you should see when you visit the https://localhost:7262/Recipe/Recipes URL In your browser in Figure 1

Recipes

Burgers
Classic beef burgers topped with fresh lettuce, ripe tomatoes, and gooey cheese. Perfect for a casual dinner or a backyard barbecue.
View Recipe

Pizza
Homemade pizza layered with savory tomato sauce, mozzarella cheese, and a selection of toppings to fit any taste. Ideal for family movie nights.
View Recipe

Spaghetti Bolognese
A hearty Italian dish featuring spaghetti topped with a meaty tomato sauce. A comfort food favorite that's both satisfying and delicious.
View Recipe

Figure 1 – The recipe details displayed in the recipes view

If you click the "View Recipe" button underneath any of the recipes, then you will be taken to the recipe details page that we created in Chapter 6; as the recipe database details are currently hardcoded on that page, you will see the same details regardless of which button is clicked. Let's fix that issue now by changing the controller code to use the *_context* object and query the database. Copy the code below over the existing *Recipe* method in your *RecipeController.cs* file

```
public IActionResult Recipe(int id) {

        var recipe = _context.Recipes.Find(id);
        if (recipe == null)
        {
                return NotFound();
        }
        return View(recipe);
}
```

Code Explanation

The Recipe function takes in an id parameter, which we use to look up the recipe details using the *Find* method of the *Recipes* objects on the *_context* object.

If the recipe variable is null, meaning that the recipe details cannot be found, we return a 404 HTTP code via the *NotFound()* function. If it is not null, we pass it back to the view.

Because the view accepts a recipe object and we are now passing a recipe object that has been populated via the database rather than one where we hard-coded the values, the view should continue to work without any further changes.

So once the view controller code is in place, and the project has been rebuilt, clicking each of the recipe buttons should show the details for that recipe, as shown in Figure 2

Burgers
Category: Main Courses

Description:
Classic beef burgers topped with fresh lettuce, ripe tomatoes, and gooey cheese. Perfect for a casual dinner or a backyard barbecue.

Instructions:
1. Grill beef patties until cooked to desired doneness.
2. Toast buns on the grill for a minute.
3. Add lettuce, tomato, cheese, and patties to buns.
4. Serve with ketchup, mustard, or your favorite burger sauce.

Figure 2 – Individual recipe details from the database

We now have code in place to list all the recipes in the database. In the next chapter, we'll extend this by adding search functionality.

Chapter 9: Adding A Search Facility

Thanks to the work we did in the last chapter, we now have the functionality to list all of the recipes in the database and to drill down into the details of each individual recipe.

As we start adding more recipes to the database, a search function would be useful so we can quickly find the ones we need.

In this chapter, we'll add the search functionality to our app.

We'll begin by making a change to the Recipes function in the *RecipeController.cs* file

```
public IActionResult Recipes(string searchString)
{
        var recipes = from r in _context.Recipes
                      select r;


        if (!string.IsNullOrEmpty(searchString))
        {
            recipes = recipes.Where(s => s.Name.ToLower().Contains(searchString.ToLower()));
        }


        return View(recipes);
}
```

Code Explanation

There are a couple of changes to the code

```
public  IActionResult Recipes(string searchString)
```

We added a searchString parameter to the recipe function

```
if (!string.IsNullOrEmpty(searchString))
        {
            recipes = recipes.Where(s =>
s.Name.ToLower().Contains(searchString.ToLower()));
}
```

If the *searchString* parameter is not null or empty, we use it to further filter the list of recipes returned from the database. We then return the collection of recipes to the view as before.

To support the controller changes we need to make some changes to the *Recipes.cshtml* view file in the *Views/Recipe* folder. The changes are in bold below

```cshtml
@model IQueryable<Recipe>

@{
    ViewBag.Title = "Recipes";
    string searchString = Context.Request.Query["searchString"];
}

<div class="container my-4">
    <h1 class="mb-3">Recipes</h1>

    <!-- Search form -->
    <form method="get" class="form-inline mb-3">
        <div class="form-group mb-2">
            <input type="text" name="searchString" class="form-control" placeholder="Search Recipes" value="@searchString"/>
        </div>
        <button type="submit" class="btn btn-primary">Search</button>
    </form>
    <!-- Recipes List -->
    <div class="row">
        @foreach (var recipe in Model)
        {
            <div class="col-md-4 mb-4">
                <div class="card h-100">
                    <img class="card-img-top" src="@recipe.ImagePath" alt="@recipe.Name">
                    <div class="card-body d-flex flex-column">
                        <h5 class="card-title">@recipe.Name</h5>
                        <p class="card-text">@recipe.Description</p>
                        <a href="@Url.Action("Recipe", "Recipe", new { id = recipe.Id })" class="btn btn-primary mt-auto">View Recipe</a>
                    </div>
```

```
            </div>
        </div>
    }
  </div>
</div>
```

Code Explanation

Let's look at what we've added to the code.

```
string searchString = Context.Request.Query["searchString"];
```

Here we capture the search string entered by the user in a variable named *searchString*.

```
<!-- Search form -->
 <form method="get" class="form-inline mb-3">
        <div class="form-group mb-2">
            <input type="text" name="searchString" class="form-control" placeholder="Search Recipes" value="@searchString"/>
        </div>
        <button type="submit" class="btn btn-primary">Search</button>
 </form>
```

We then add an HTML form for the user to input their search phrase. We use the searchString variable created in the previous step to populate the searchString textbox with the value entered for the current search.

Because the *searchString* textbox has a name that corresponds to the searchString parameter we added to the Recipes function in the Recipe Controller, its value is automatically passed to the function and can be used in the search.

Now, the https://localhost:7262/recipe/Recipes page contains a search field, and when we enter text into the field the search results are changed accordingly.

Figure 1 – Search results on the recipe page

Adding a Category Search

Now that we have a title search in place, we're going to add a category field search as well. Rather than letting the user just type in a category, we're going to add a drop-down menu so they can only search by categories that are already in our database. To populate a drop-down menu, we'll need to pass a list of categories from the controller to the view.

This presents us with a problem: up until now, we have only needed to pass one piece of information to the view, which has either been the recipe data or a list of recipes for the search page to show. Now we need to pass on two things

- The list of recipes returned by the search
- The list of categories for the drop-down

To solve this problem, we're going to introduce a view model; this will be a model that has two properties, one for the list of recipes and one for the category list. To do this we'll add a file named *RecipeSearchViewModel.cs* to the *Models* folder and then add the following code

```
using Microsoft.AspNetCore.Mvc.Rendering;
namespace RecipeDatabase.Models
{
    public class RecipeSearchViewModel
    {
        public SelectList Categories { get; set; }
        public List<Recipe> Recipes { get; set; }
    }
}
```

Now that we have the model, we can alter our controller code to handle a category in the search parameters and also pass the list of categories for the drop-down over to the view via the view model. Copy the code below over the existing *Recipes* function in the *RecipeController.cs* file. I've highlighted any new code in bold.

```csharp
public IActionResult Recipes(string searchString, string recipeCategory)
{
    // Use LINQ to get a list of categories for filtering
    IQueryable<string> categoryQuery = from r in _context.Recipes
                                       where r.Category != string.Empty
                                       orderby r.Category
                                       select r.Category;

    var recipes = from r in _context.Recipes
                  select r;

    if (!string.IsNullOrEmpty(searchString))
    {
        recipes = recipes.Where(s => s.Name.ToLower().Contains(searchString.ToLower()));
    }

    if (!string.IsNullOrEmpty(recipeCategory))
    {
        recipes = recipes.Where(x => x.Category == recipeCategory);
    }

    var categories = categoryQuery.Distinct().ToList()
        .Select(c => new Microsoft.AspNetCore.Mvc.Rendering.SelectListItem
        {
            Value = c,
            Text = c,
            Selected = c == recipeCategory
        });
```

```
            var recipeSearchViewModel = new RecipeSearchViewModel
            {
                Categories = new Microsoft.AspNetCore.Mvc.Rendering.SelectList(categories, "Value", "Text", recipeCategory),
                Recipes = recipes.ToList()
            };

            return View(recipeSearchViewModel);
}
```

Code Explanation

To enable us to perform the category search we pass the category value into the function

`public IActionResult Recipes(string searchString, string recipeCategory)`

We then add a LINQ query to get the categories to populate the drop-down

```
IQueryable<string> categoryQuery = from r in _context.Recipes
                                   where r.Category != string.Empty
                                   orderby r.Category
                                   select r.Category;
```

Because there is only one table in our database we don't have a categories table, so we need to work out the categories from the Recipe table.

It could be argued that a separate categories table would have been a better choice, but I wanted to keep things as simple as possible for the purposes of the book. This topic will come up again when we look at the recipe creation functionality in the next chapter.

We then add some code similar to the title search code to filter the list of recipes based on the category search value,

```
if (!string.IsNullOrEmpty(recipeCategory))
{
    recipes = recipes.Where(x => x.Category == recipeCategory);
}
```

In order to get the items to populate our drop-down, we build up a collection of select list items to pass over to the view. We mark the last category item that we searched for as Selected so that when the search results are returned, the user can clearly see what category was used to perform the search. Note that we use the LINQ *Distinct()* function to reduce the list to only unique categories. This prevents category names from appearing more than once in the drop-down.

```
var categories = categoryQuery.Distinct().ToList()
          .Select(c => new Microsoft.AspNetCore.Mvc.Rendering.SelectListItem
          {
              Value = c,
              Text = c,
              Selected = c == recipeCategory
          });
```

Finally, we convert the list of items to a select list and pass that and the list of recipes back to the view via the view model.

```
var recipeSearchViewModel = new RecipeSearchViewModel
{
              Categories = new Microsoft.AspNetCore.Mvc.Rendering.SelectList(categories, "Value", "Text", recipeCategory),
              Recipes = recipes.ToList()
};


return View(recipeSearchViewModel);
```

Altering the view code for the category search

Now that the controller code is in place, we can examine altering the view code. Copy the code below into the *Recipes.cshtml* file in the *Views/Recipe* folder, replacing any existing code. Once again, I've highlighted any new code in bold.

```cshtml
@model RecipeDatabase.Models.RecipeSearchViewModel

@{
    ViewBag.Title = "Recipes";
    string searchString = Context.Request.Query["searchString"];
}


<div class="container my-4">
    <h1 class="mb-3">Recipes</h1>


    <!-- Search form -->
    <form method="get" class="form-inline mb-3"
        <div class="form-group mb-2">
            <input type="text" name="searchString" class="form-control" placeholder="Search Recipes" value="@searchString"/>
        </div>
        <div class="form-group mb-2">
            <select class="form-control" asp-items="Model.Categories" name="recipeCategory">
                <option value="">All Categories</option>
            </select>
        </div>
        <button type="submit" class="btn btn-primary">Search</button>
    </form>

    <div class="mb-2">
        @Model.Recipes.Count recipes returned.
    </div>


    <!-- Recipes List -->
    <div class="row">
```

```html
            @foreach (var recipe in Model.Recipes)
            {
                <div class="col-md-4 mb-4">
                    <div class="card h-100">
                        <img class="card-img-top" src="@recipe.ImagePath" alt="@recipe.Name">
                        <div class="card-body d-flex flex-column">
                            <h5 class="card-title">@recipe.Name</h5>
                            <p class="card-text">@recipe.Description</p>
                            <a href="@Url.Action("Recipe", "Recipe", new { id = recipe.Id })" class="btn btn-primary mt-auto">View Recipe</a>
                        </div>
                    </div>
                </div>
            }
        </div>
</div>
```

Code Explanation

Our view model has now changed to the view model we added earlier

`@model RecipeDatabase.Models.RecipeSearchViewModel`

We add the form field for the Category search and bind the select list HTML element to the category collection that we created in the controller and passed into the view using the view model. We use the *asp-items* property to do this.

```html
        <div class="form-group mb-2">
            <select class="form-control" asp-items="Model.Categories" name="recipeCategory">
                <option value="">All Categories</option>
            </select>
        </div>
```

We also added a property to show us how many results have been returned by the search

```
<div class="mb-2">
    @Model.Recipes.Count recipes returned.
</div>
```

Now when we run a search, results are returned based on the criteria entered by the user, as shown in Figure 2.

Recipes

ag

Main Courses

[Search]

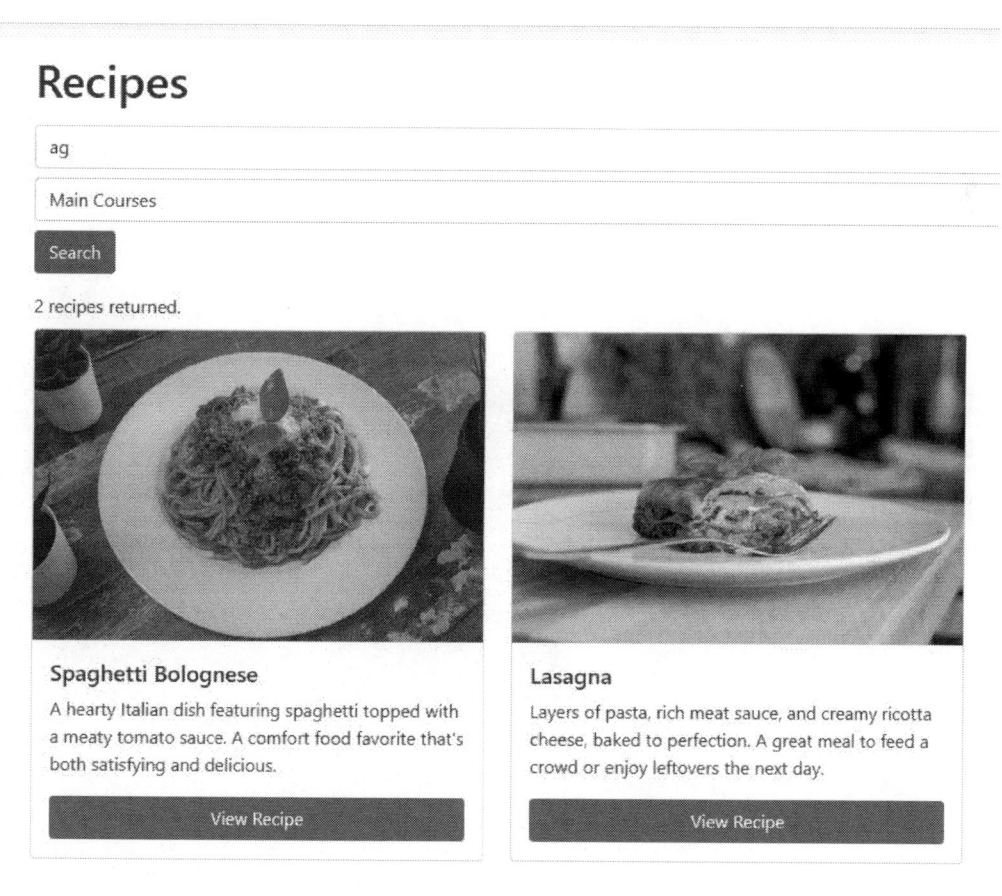

2 recipes returned.

Spaghetti Bolognese
A hearty Italian dish featuring spaghetti topped with a meaty tomato sauce. A comfort food favorite that's both satisfying and delicious.
[View Recipe]

Lasagna
Layers of pasta, rich meat sauce, and creamy ricotta cheese, baked to perfection. A great meal to feed a crowd or enjoy leftovers the next day.
[View Recipe]

Figure 2 – a search using title and category

Chapter 10: Extending the Model

The ASP.NET MVC framework allows us to extend Models with attributes. These attributes can then be used to add functionality, like display code and automatic validation.

I haven't mentioned these attributes yet, so we'll just take a quick look at them now in this short chapter. Here's our model code with some attributes added.

```
using System.ComponentModel;
using System.ComponentModel.DataAnnotations;

namespace RecipeDatabase.Models
{
    public class Recipe
    {
        public int Id { get; set; }
        [Required]
        public string Name { get; set; }
        [Required]
        public string Category { get; set; }
        [Required]
        public string ImagePath { get; set; }
        [Required]
        public string Description { get; set; }
        [DisplayName("Recipe Instructions")]
        [Required]
        public string RecipeInstructions { get; set; }
    }
}
```

As you can see from the code above, we've added the

[Required]

Attribute to all the properties in the model apart from the id property (which the Entity Framework uses to identify and track the models/recipes in the database). This means when we try to submit a form with values missing for these fields, the baked-in validation code will inform us that values need to be added. You can see this functionality in action on the Recipe Create screen in Figure 1

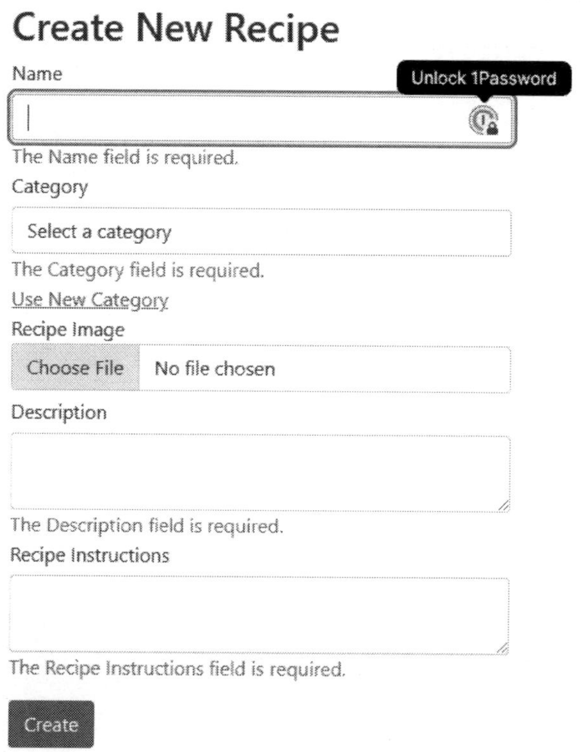

Create New Recipe

Name

[The Name field is required.]

Category

[Select a category]

The Category field is required.

Use New Category

Recipe Image

[Choose File] No file chosen

Description

[textarea]

The Description field is required.

Recipe Instructions

[textarea]

The Recipe Instructions field is required.

[Create]

Figure 1 The recipe creation screen informs us that data is missing

Aside from the *Required* attribute we also use the *DisplayName* attribute, by default when the framework renders a form field using code like this

```
<div class="form-group">
    <label asp-for="RecipeInstructions" class="control-label"></label>
    <textarea asp-for="RecipeInstructions" class="form-control"></textarea>
    <span asp-validation-for="RecipeInstructions" class="text-danger"></span>
</div>
```

It will populate the label with the property name from the c# model class, as our Recipe Instructions property name contains two words merged together, we can make the label more readable by adding the

```
[DisplayName("Recipe Instructions")]
```

attribute.

Model State

When we start coding the create, edit and delete functionality in the next few chapters we will often see code like this

```
if (ModelState.IsValid)
{
        //model processing code here
}
```

ModelState is a feature used by the ASP.NET MVC framework to check if the data in the model is valid before performing further operations with it, such as saving it to a database.

There are two primary methods of data validation in the MVC framework:

Client Side

To enable client-side validation, you can include the following script section at the bottom of your view file

```
@section Scripts {
    @{await Html.RenderPartialAsync("_ValidationScriptsPartial");}
}
```

This code instructs the framework to generate JavaScript code that checks the model's validity before it is posted to the server and processed by a controller. Client-side validation helps improve user experience by providing immediate feedback on input errors without the need to wait for a server response.

Server Side

While client-side validation is useful, it's important to have server-side validation as well for several reasons

- Users may have turned off Javascript in their browsers
- There might be an issue with the client-side validation that caused it not to fire
- Malicious attackers may find a way to bypass the client-side validation

To implement server-side validation, we use *ModelState.IsValid* to check the validity of the model. If this check fails, it's essential to return the model back to the view, along with any validation errors stored in ModelState, so that the errors can be displayed to the user.

As we start adding the Create functionality in the next chapter, you'll see how we implement client and server-side Model State validation in our code.

In this chapter we've taken a very brief look at model attributes if you want more information there is a much more comprehensive write-up here
https://learn.microsoft.com/en-us/aspnet/core/mvc/models/validation?view=aspnetcore-8.0#data-annotations

Chapter 11: Adding The Create Recipe Functionality

Now that we have the recipe search functionality in place, we'll turn our attention to the functionality that allows users to add new recipes to the database. In subsequent chapters, we'll also look at edit and delete functionality.

To start with this let's look at the view functionality, we'll add a view named *Create.cshtml* to the *Views/Recipe* folder and add the code below

```
@model RecipeDatabase.Models.Recipe


@{
    ViewData["Title"] = "Create Recipe";
    string newCategory = Context.Request.Query["newCategory"];
}


<h2>Create New Recipe</h2>


<div class="row">
    <div class="col-md-4">
        <form method="post" asp-controller="Recipe" asp-action="Create" enctype="multipart/form-data">
            <div asp-validation-summary="ModelOnly" class="text-danger"></div>
            <div class="form-group">
                <label asp-for="Name" class="control-label"></label>
                <input asp-for="Name" class="form-control" />
                <span asp-validation-for="Name" class="text-danger"></span>
            </div>
            @if (newCategory == "true") {
```

```html
            <div class="form-group">
                <label asp-for="Category" class="control-label"></label>
                <input asp-for="Category" class="form-control" />
                <span asp-validation-for="Category" class="text-danger"></span>
            </div>
            @Html.ActionLink("Use Existing Category", "Create", "Recipe")
        }
        else {
            <div class="form-group">
                <label asp-for="Category" class="control-label"></label>
                @Html.DropDownListFor(
                    m => m.Category,
                    (IEnumerable<SelectListItem>)ViewData["Categories"],
                    "Select a category",
                    new { @class = "form-control" }
                )
                <span asp-validation-for="Category" class="text-danger"></span>
            </div>
            @Html.ActionLink("Use New Category", "Create", "Recipe", new { newCategory = "true" })
        }
        <div class="form-group">
            <label for="ImagePath">Recipe Image</label>
            <input type="file" class="form-control" name="ImagePath" />
        </div>
        <div class="form-group">
            <label asp-for="Description" class="control-label"></label>
            <textarea asp-for="Description" class="form-control"></textarea>
```

```
            <span asp-validation-for="Description" class="text-
danger"></span>

        </div>

        <div class="form-group mb-2">

            <label asp-for="RecipeInstructions" class="control-
label"></label>

            <textarea asp-for="RecipeInstructions" class="form-
control"></textarea>

            <span asp-validation-for="RecipeInstructions" class="text-
danger"></span>

        </div>

        <button type="submit" class="btn btn-primary">Create</button>

    </form>

  </div>

</div>


@section Scripts {

    @{await Html.RenderPartialAsync("_ValidationScriptsPartial");}

}
```

Code Explanation

```
<form method="post" asp-controller="Recipe" asp-action="Create"
enctype="multipart/form-data">
```

Although the opening form tag looks similar to form tags we have used in other chapters you may have noticed that we have added the *enctype="multipart/form-data"* attribute. This has been added to allow us to handle the image upload form element that we have on the form as shown in Figure 1

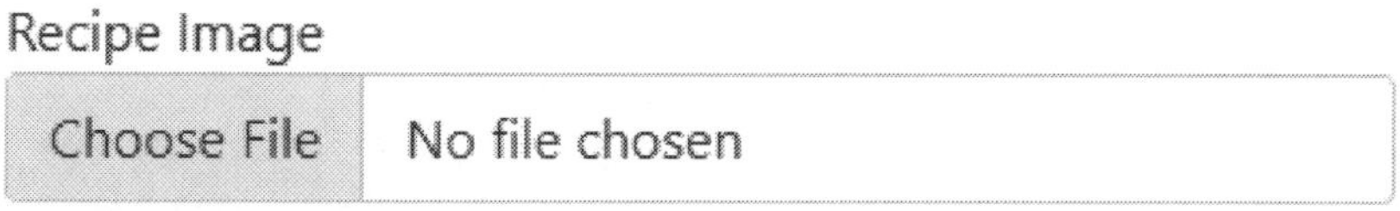

Figure 1 – the image upload component on the form

```
            <div class="form-group">
                <label asp-for="Category" class="control-label"></label>
                @Html.DropDownListFor(
                    m => m.Category,
                    (IEnumerable<SelectListItem>)ViewData["Categories"],
                    "Select a category",
                    new { @class = "form-control" }
                )
                <span asp-validation-for="Category" class="text-danger"></span>
            </div>
```

Even though we are populating a category drop-down as we did for the search facility in the previous chapter, we have not used a view model; instead, we have passed the Categories list using the *ViewData*. We're doing it this way because it simplifies form submissions by allowing us to directly bind a recipe object to the form. This setup allows ASP.NET MVC to automatically handle form data, keeping our view straightforward and focused.

The next section of code allows the user to use an existing category or create a new one

```
@if (newCategory == "true") {
            <div class="form-group">
                <label asp-for="Category" class="control-label"></label>
                <input asp-for="Category" class="form-control" />
                <span asp-validation-for="Category" class="text-danger"></span>
            </div>
            @Html.ActionLink("Use Existing Category", "Create", "Recipe")
        }
        else {
            <div class="form-group">
                <label asp-for="Category" class="control-label"></label>
                @Html.DropDownListFor(
```

```
                m => m.Category,
                (IEnumerable<SelectListItem>)ViewData["Categories"],
                "Select a category",
                new { @class = "form-control" }
                )
            <span asp-validation-for="Category" class="text-danger"></span>
        </div>
        @Html.ActionLink("Use New Category", "Create", "Recipe", new { newCategory = "true" })
}
```

This if statement is designed to allow a user to either
- Choose from an existing category for their new recipe
- Create a new category to use with their new recipe

Because our database only has one table (the Recipes table), we do not have a separate categories table. If we did have the categories in their own table, then we could have written some CRUD functionality for Categories, and the user could have used that to add a new category and then come back to the recipe creation screen to use their new category.

I wanted to avoid doing that for the purposes of the book as I thought it would lead to writing repetitive create/edit delete code so I've used an alternate method where we

- Add both a category drop-down and a category text field to the Create form
- Add links close to both input fields that link back to the create screen with a query string parameter that details whether we should use a new category or not
- Added an if statement around both of the category input methods, depending on the value passed back by the query string parameter, either the drop-down or the text field will be displayed on the screen

```
@Html.ActionLink("Use New Category", "Create", "Recipe", new { newCategory = "true" })
```

This is the code we use to build the link. We use the built-in *HTML.ActionLink* method and point the link at the Create view on the Recipe controller. We use the route values parameter of the *Html.ActionLink* to pass in

```
new { newCategory = "true" })
```

This will add a query string parameter to the link URL, so it will end up looking something like this

https://localhost:7262/Recipe/Create?newCategory=true

We then read the *newCategory* value at the top of the page using this code

```
@{
    ViewData["Title"] = "Create Recipe";
    string newCategory = Context.Request.Query["newCategory"];
}
```

And then we use the *newCategory* variable in the if statement to determine which of the two form fields we show to the user.

The Controller Code

Now let's take a look at the controller code

For the Create, Edit and Post functionality the controller code will follow a similar pattern, there will be two methods in the recipe class for each controller and the methods will be
- A method that sets up the initial form
- A method that processes any user input, updates the database accordingly and then informs the user that their changes have been made.

The second method will always have an *[HttpPost]* attribute above it that informs the framework that it should be used after the form has been posted.

Let's take a look at the controller method that initially sets up the Create form, you'll need to copy the code below into the *RecipeController.cs* file inside the *Controllers* folder

```
public IActionResult Create()
{
        IQueryable<string> categoryQuery = from r in _context.Recipes
                                    where r.Category != string.Empty
                                    orderby r.Category
                                    select r.Category;

        var categories = categoryQuery.Distinct().ToList()
        .Select(c => new Microsoft.AspNetCore.Mvc.Rendering.SelectListItem
        {
                Value = c,
                Text = c,
        });
        ViewData["Categories"] = categories;

        return View();
}
```

Code Explanation

The code that sets up the create input screen is relatively straightforward. We have a query that gets the category data, and as discussed earlier in the chapter, we convert that to a collection of *SelectListItems* and then pass it along to the view using the *ViewData* dictionary.

We will need the code that gets the categories and writes into the *ViewData* in multiple places in the create and edit functionality so let's create a function that allows us to reuse the code, and copy the function below into the *RecipeController.cs* file

```
private void WriteCategoriesIntoViewData() {
        IQueryable<string> categoryQuery = from r in _context.Recipes
                                    where r.Category != string.Empty
                                    orderby r.Category
                                    select r.Category;

        var categories = categoryQuery.Distinct().ToList()
        .Select(c => new Microsoft.AspNetCore.Mvc.Rendering.SelectListItem
        {
                Value = c,
                Text = c,
        });
        ViewData["Categories"] = categories;
}
```

We can now simplify our controller code using the function, replace the *Create* action result function in your *RecipeController.cs* file with the one below

```
public IActionResult Create()
{
        WriteCategoriesIntoViewData();
        return View();
}
```

Once the controller and view code are in place, the create form should look like Figure 1 when viewed in the browser.

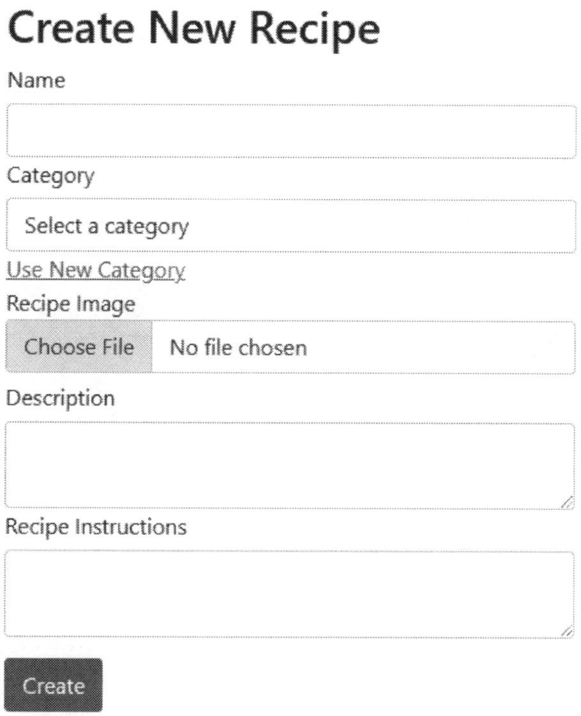

Create New Recipe

Name

Category

Select a category

Use New Category

Recipe Image

Choose File   No file chosen

Description

Recipe Instructions

Create

Figure 1 – the create form

Now let's take a look at the method that processes the data posted by the create form

```
[HttpPost]
[ValidateAntiForgeryToken]
public IActionResult
Create([Bind("Name,Slug,Category,ImagePath,Description,RecipeInstructions")]
Recipe recipe, IFormFile ImagePath)
        {
            if (ModelState.IsValid)
            {
                if (ImagePath != null && ImagePath.Length > 0)
                {
                    var fileName = Path.GetFileName(ImagePath.FileName);
                    var filePath = Path.Combine(Directory.GetCurrentDirectory(), "wwwroot/images", fileName);

                    using (var fileStream = new FileStream(filePath, FileMode.Create))
                    {
                        ImagePath.CopyTo(fileStream);
                    }

                    // Save the file path relative to the wwwroot
                    recipe.ImagePath = $"/images/{fileName}";
                }

                _context.Add(recipe);
                _context.SaveChanges();
                return RedirectToAction("Recipe", "Recipe", new { id = recipe.Id });
            }
            WriteCategoriesIntoViewData();
            return View(recipe);
        }
```

Code Explanation

```
[HttpPost]
[ValidateAntiForgeryToken]
public IActionResult
Create([Bind("Name,Slug,Category,ImagePath,Description,RecipeInstructions")]
Recipe recipe, IFormFile ImagePath)
```

As mentioned previously, the function is marked with the *[HttpPost]* attribute to indicate that it should be run in response to the form in the *Create.cshtml* view code posting its data to the server.

The *[ValidateAntiForgeryToken]* is a security feature. It helps protect the data being submitted through forms from malicious attacks, ensuring that the information sent to the server is from the user and not from an outsider trying to trick the system. It's a bit beyond the scope of this book to go into any more detail than that, but you can read more here https://learn.microsoft.com/en-us/aspnet/web-api/overview/security/preventing-cross-site-request-forgery-csrf-attacks

The Bind statement that appears alongside the parameters of the *Create* function tells the framework which of the form fields should be bound to the recipe object, we also define an *IFormFile* variable named *ImagePath* which will contain the details about the uploaded image

```
if (ImagePath != null && ImagePath.Length > 0)
            {
                    var fileName = Path.GetFileName(ImagePath.FileName);
                    var filePath = Path.Combine(Directory.GetCurrentDirectory(), "wwwroot/images", fileName);

                    using (var fileStream = new FileStream(filePath, FileMode.Create))
                    {
                            await ImagePath.CopyTo(fileStream);
                    }

                    // Save the file path relative to the wwwroot
                    recipe.ImagePath = $"/images/{fileName}";
            }
```

This is the code that handles the uploaded image, here's what it does

1. Performs a check to see that we have data in the *ImagePath* variable, if the variable doesn't contain data then we have no image data to save so no further action is taken
2. If we have data in the *ImagePath* variable, then the code gets the uploaded image's file name and then appends the *wwwroot/images* directory path to it. We're going to store the image in the *wwwrooot* folder as that is the best place to store static files, as discussed in Chapter 3
3. The code then saves the image to the path worked out in the previous step using the *ImagePath.CopyTo* method
4. Finally the code saves the new path to the *ImagePath* property of the recipe object

Once the image has been successfully processed, the rest of the recipe data has already been bound to the *recipe* object by the Asp.Net framework's binding functionality, so we are able to add the recipe object to the _context object and then save it using the *SaveChanges* method.

```
_context.Add(recipe);
_context.SaveChanges();
```

Once the recipe data has been saved to the database, we use the *RedirectToAction* method to take the user to the Recipe view on the Recipe controller which will show the user all the details of the new recipe.

If the *ModelState.IsValid* check fails, then we re-add the Category information to the *ViewData* and pass the failing recipe model back to the view. This should allow the view to display any *ModelState* errors that have been returned

```
WriteCategoriesIntoViewData();
return View(recipe);
```

You can see how this would look to the user in Figure 2 and Figure 3.

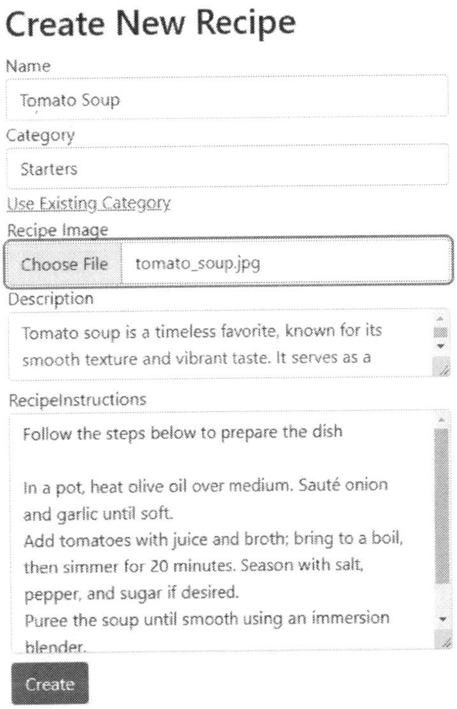

Figure 2 – New recipe data entered into the Create screen

Tomato Soup

Category: Starters

Description:
Tomato soup is a timeless favorite, known for its smooth texture and vibrant taste. It serves as a comforting meal or a delightful starter.

Instructions:
Follow the steps below to prepare the dish

In a pot, heat olive oil over medium. Sauté onion and garlic until soft.
Add tomatoes with juice and broth; bring to a boil, then simmer for 20 minutes. Season with salt, pepper, and sugar if desired.
Puree the soup until smooth using an immersion blender.
Serve hot, garnished with basil.

Figure 3 – The new recipe shown in the recipe screen after the "Create" button has been clicked.

Chapter 12: Adding Edit Functionality

In the last chapter, we examined the Create functionality; now that we have that in place, let's examine editing recipes.

As with the create functionality in the last chapter, we'll start by looking at the view code. Create a view named *Edit.cshtml* in the *Views/Recipe* folder and add the following code

```
@model RecipeDatabase.Models.Recipe

@{
    ViewData["Title"] = "Edit Recipe";
}

<h1>Edit Recipe</h1>

<h4>Recipe</h4>
<hr />
<div class="row">
    <div class="col-md-4">
        <form asp-action="Edit"  enctype="multipart/form-data">
            <div asp-validation-summary="ModelOnly" class="text-danger"></div>
            <input type="hidden" asp-for="Id" />
            <div class="form-group">
                <label asp-for="Name" class="control-label"></label>
                <input asp-for="Name" class="form-control" />
                <span asp-validation-for="Name" class="text-danger"></span>
            </div>
            <div class="form-group">
                <label asp-for="Category" class="control-label"></label>
                @Html.DropDownListFor(
                        m => m.Category,
                        (IEnumerable<SelectListItem>)ViewData["Categories"],
                        "Select a category",
                        new { @class = "form-control" }
                        )
                <span asp-validation-for="Category" class="text-danger"></span>
            </div>
            <div class="form-group">
                <label for="ImagePath">Recipe Image</label>
                @if (!string.IsNullOrEmpty(Model.ImagePath))
                {
                    <img src="@Url.Content(Model.ImagePath)" alt="Current Image" class="img-thumbnail" />
```

```html
                        <input type="hidden" id="ImagePathOld" name="ImagePathOld" value="@Model.ImagePath" />
                    }
                    <input type="checkbox" id="changeFile" name="ChangeFile" />
                    <label for="changeFile">Change file</label>
                </div>
                <div id="fileInputContainer" style="display: none;">
                    <input type="file" class="form-control" name="ImagePathNew"/>
                </div>
                <div class="form-group">
                    <label asp-for="Description" class="control-label"></label>
                    <textarea asp-for="Description" class="form-control"></textarea>
                    <span asp-validation-for="Description" class="text-danger"></span>
                </div>
                <div class="form-group">
                    <label asp-for="RecipeInstructions" class="control-label"></label>
                    <textarea asp-for="RecipeInstructions" class="form-control"></textarea>
                    <span asp-validation-for="RecipeInstructions" class="text-danger"></span>
                </div>
                <div class="form-group">
                    <input type="submit" value="Save" class="btn btn-primary" />
                    <a asp-action="Index" class="btn btn-secondary">Back to List</a>
                </div>
        </form>
    </div>
</div>

@section Scripts {
    @{await Html.RenderPartialAsync("_ValidationScriptsPartial");}
    <script>
        $(document).ready(function () {
            $('#changeFile').change(function () {
                if ($(this).is(':checked')) {
                    $('#fileInputContainer').show();
                } else {
                    $('#fileInputContainer').hide();
                }
            });
        });
    </script>
}
```

Code Explanation

You've probably noticed that this code is similar to the create code in the last chapter; we are using the same functionality to bind the Categories to a drop-down list.

We use the strongly typed model to populate the form with data, because we are doing it this way, we can use code like this

```
<div class="form-group">
    <label asp-for="Name" class="control-label"></label>
    <input asp-for="Name" class="form-control" />
    <span asp-validation-for="Name" class="text-danger"></span>
</div>
```

Here, the *asp-for* tag helper automatically populates the label and form fields with the relevant model information for the Name property; a similar pattern is used to populate the form fields for the other Recipe object properties.

One significant difference is how we have to handle the image field, we can't populate the file dialogue with the previously held value as we have no way of knowing where the image is held on the user's machine, so we initially just show the image and then give the user the option of changing it if they require by checking a check box as shown in Figures 1 and 2

Figure 1 - The change file checkbox

110

Recipe Image

[Image of spaghetti dish on a plate]

☑ Change file

[Choose File] No file chosen

Figure 2 - the file dialog field that appears when the change file checkbox is checked

To handle this logic, we use the following HTML mark-up

```
<div class="form-group">
            <label for="ImagePath">Recipe Image</label>
            @if (!string.IsNullOrEmpty(Model.ImagePath))
            {
                <img src="@Url.Content(Model.ImagePath)" alt="Current Image" class="img-thumbnail" />
                <input type="hidden" id="ImagePathOld" name="ImagePathOld" value="@Model.ImagePath" />
            }
            <input type="checkbox" id="changeFile" name="ChangeFile" />
            <label for="changeFile">Change file</label>
        </div>
        <div id="fileInputContainer" style="display: none;">
            <input type="file" class="form-control" name="ImagePathNew"/>
        </div>
```

111

In the markup, we define an *img* element that shows the currently chosen image and a hidden form field that holds the location of the chosen image. We then add the checkbox and a hidden div that holds the file select input field.

The jQuery code below controls the hiding and showing of the file input dialog. Note that we can use the jQuery framework without adding a reference to it, as it is already included in the master layout file.

```
<script>
$(document).ready(function () {
        $('#changeFile').change(function () {
                if ($(this).is(':checked')) {
                        $('#fileInputContainer').show();
                } else {
                        $('#fileInputContainer').hide();
                }
        });
});
</script>
```

The jQuery function fires when the *ChangeFile* checkbox is clicked. If the checkbox is checked, it shows the *fileInputContainer* div that contains the file input dialog. If the checkbox is unchecked, the div is hidden again.

When the form is submitted, we'll be able to check the file dialog value and the hidden field value and decide which to save to our model.

We'll see how we handle this logic when the form is submitted soon, but for now, we'll look at the controller method that handles the initial display of the edit form. Add the code below to the *RecipeController.cs* file in the *Controllers* folder

```
public IActionResult Edit(int? id)
{
        if (id == null)
        {
                return NotFound();
        }

        var recipe = _context.Recipes.Find(id);
        if (recipe == null)
        {
                return NotFound();
        }

        WriteCategoriesIntoViewData();
```

```
        return View(recipe);
}
```

Code Explanation

The code here is very similar to the code we used to display the create form. The only major difference is that we find the recipe in the database and pass it to the view so the edit fields are already pre-populated. We also use the model's Category property to ensure that the correct category is chosen in the Categories checkbox.

We'll now take a look at the controller method that handles the submission of the form data. Copy the method below into the *RecipeController.cs* file inside the *Controllers* directory

```
[HttpPost]
[ValidateAntiForgeryToken]
public IActionResult Edit(int id,
[Bind("Id,Name,Slug,Category,Description,RecipeInstructions")] Recipe recipe,
string ImagePathOld, IFormFile ImagePathNew)
{
        if (id != recipe.Id)
        {
                return NotFound();
        }

        if (ImagePathNew == null || ImagePathNew.Length == 0)
        {
                ModelState.Remove("ImagePathNew");
        }

        if (ModelState.IsValid)
        {
                if (ImagePathNew != null && ImagePathNew.Length > 0)
                {
                        var fileName = Path.GetFileName(ImagePathNew.FileName);
                        var filePath = Path.Combine(Directory.GetCurrentDirectory(), "wwwroot/images", fileName);

                        using (var fileStream = new FileStream(filePath, FileMode.Create))
                        {
                                ImagePathNew.CopyTo(fileStream);
                        }

                        // Save the file path relative to the wwwroot
                        recipe.ImagePath = $"/images/{fileName}";
```

```
        }
        else {
                recipe.ImagePath = ImagePathOld;
        }

        _context.Update(recipe);
        _context.SaveChanges();

        return RedirectToAction("Recipe", "Recipe", new { id = recipe.Id });
    }

    WriteCategoriesIntoViewData();
    return View(recipe);

}
```

Code Explanation

Let's take a look at how the image save code is handled

```
[HttpPost]
[ValidateAntiForgeryToken]
public IActionResult Edit(int id,
[Bind("Id,Name,Slug,Category,Description,RecipeInstructions")] Recipe recipe,
string ImagePathOld, IFormFile ImagePathNew)
```

The code above is similar to the *HttpPost* method we looked at for the create functionality, as you can see, we are binding a number of different values from the form

- The id parameter represents the Id of the recipe being edited. It is passed as a separate parameter and is typically obtained from the URL or the *id* route parameter.
- The recipe parameter represents the Recipe model being edited. The [Bind] attribute specifies which properties of the Recipe model should be bound from the form data. In this case, only the properties listed within the [Bind] attribute (Id, Name, Slug, Category, Description and RecipeInstructions) will be populated with the values submitted in the form. This is a security measure to prevent something called "over-posting attacks", where additional properties not intended to be updated could be included in the form data.
- The *ImagePathOld* parameter represents the existing image path from the recipe, which is passed as a separate parameter from the form data.
- The *ImagePathNew* parameter represents the new image file that may have been uploaded during the editing process (if the user has opted to change the existing

image and has uploaded a new image via the file upload form field). As with the Create functionality, we use an *IFormFile* type to handle this value.

The code then checks to see that we are trying to update a valid recipe

```
if (id != recipe.Id)
{
        return NotFound();
}
```

This if statement is a security check to ensure that the *id* parameter provided in the URL or route parameter matches the *Id* value submitted in the form data (*recipe.Id*).

- If the *id* parameter from the URL does not match the *recipe.Id* value from the form data means the requested recipe ID and the ID of the recipe being edited do not match up.
- If this is the case, the *NotFound()* method is returned, indicating that the requested recipe was not found or that the request was invalid.

This check helps prevent scenarios where a user may attempt to manipulate the URL or form data to edit a recipe they are not authorized to modify. By comparing the id from the URL with the *recipe.Id* from the form data, the application ensures that the user is editing the intended recipe and not trying to access or modify a different recipe.

We then check to see if the new image field has been populated, if it hasn't then we remove the '*ImagePathNew*' value from the *ModelState* collection as we do not need to check it if it hasn't been used

```
if (ImagePathNew == null || ImagePathNew.Length == 0)
{
    ModelState.Remove("ImagePathNew");
}
```

Following the *ModelState* check, we check which of the image fields are populated

```
if (ImagePathNew != null && ImagePathNew.Length > 0)
{
        var fileName = Path.GetFileName(ImagePathNew.FileName);
        var filePath = Path.Combine(Directory.GetCurrentDirectory(), "wwwroot/images", fileName);

        using (var fileStream = new FileStream(filePath, FileMode.Create))
        {
```

```
                ImagePathNew.CopyTo(fileStream);
        }

        // Save the file path relative to the wwwroot
        recipe.ImagePath = $"/images/{fileName}";
}
else {
        recipe.ImagePath = ImagePathOld;
}
```

The code uses an if statement. If the *ImagePathNew* variable is populated (meaning that the file dialog has been populated), we use the file dialog value and save the details of the image to the server as we did with the create code in the previous chapter. If the *ImagePathNew* variable does not contain a value, we use the value of the *ImagePathOld* variable, which is taken from the hidden field on the form.

As with the Create code, we add the updated recipe to the *_context* and then save the updated details using the *SaveChanges* method. We then redirect the user to the recipe details screen for their edited recipe so they can see the changes they have made.

```
_context.Update(recipe);
_context.SaveChanges();

return RedirectToAction("Recipe", "Recipe", new { id = recipe.Id });
```

As with the Create functionality, if we do have any *ModelState* errors, then we send the user back to the Edit view where the *ModelState* errors should be displayed to them.

Chapter 13: Adding Delete Functionality

In the last two chapters, we created the functionality for creating and editing recipes. In this chapter, we're going to complete the set by implementing the recipe delete function.

We'll start by creating a file named *Delete.cshtml* in the *Views/Recipe* folder, once the file has been created, copy the code below into it.

```
@model RecipeDatabase.Models.Recipe

<h2>Delete</h2>

<h3>Are you sure you want to delete this?</h3>
<div>
    <h4>Recipe</h4>
    <hr />
    <dl class="row">
        <dt class="col-sm-2">
            @Html.DisplayNameFor(model => model.Name)
        </dt>
        <dd class="col-sm-10">
            @Html.DisplayFor(model => model.Name)
        </dd>
        <dt class="col-sm-2">
            @Html.DisplayNameFor(model => model.Description)
        </dt>
        <dd class="col-sm-10">
            @Html.DisplayFor(model => model.Description)
        </dd>
    </dl>

    <form asp-controller="Recipe" asp-action="Delete" method="post">
        <input type="hidden" asp-for="Id" />
        <button type="submit" class="btn btn-danger">Delete</button>
        @Html.ActionLink("Back to List", "Recipes", "Recipe", routeValues: null, new { @class = "btn btn-secondary" })
    </form>
</div>
```

Unlike the Create and Edit views, we're not setting up a lot of form fields for the Delete view. Instead, we show the user some details about the recipe and ask them to confirm whether they want to delete it or not.

Here's what the user will be presented with on deleting a recipe

Delete	
Are you sure you want to delete this?	
Recipe	
Name	Pizza
Description	Homemade pizza layered with savory tomato sauce, mozzarella cheese, and a selection of toppings to fit any taste. Ideal for family movie nights.

Delete   Back to List

Figure 1 – The delete recipe screen

As you can see from Figure 1, the user is presented with further details about the recipe and is given the choice of either deleting it or returning to the recipe list.

The controller code to display the delete screen is below, copy it into your *RecipeController.cs* file in the *Controllers* folder

```
public IActionResult Delete(int? id)
{
        if (id == null)
        {
                return NotFound();
        }

        var recipe = _context.Recipes
                .FirstOrDefault(m => m.Id == id);

        if (recipe == null)
        {
                return NotFound();
        }

        return View(recipe);
}
```

Code Explanation

In this code, we use the *_context* object to query the database for the relevant Recipe details. The method looks up the recipe by its ID. If no recipe is found, it returns a *NotFound* result. Otherwise, it passes the recipe to the Delete view, where the user can confirm the deletion.

Now let's take a look at the code that handles the actual delete of the recipe from the database, when the user clicks the "Delete" button and the form is submitted

```
[HttpPost, ActionName("Delete")]
[ValidateAntiForgeryToken]
public IActionResult DeleteConfirmed(int id)
{
        var recipe = _context.Recipes.Find(id);
        if (recipe != null)
        {
                _context.Recipes.Remove(recipe);
                _context.SaveChanges();
                TempData["RecipeRemoved"] = recipe.Name;
        }
        return RedirectToAction(nameof(Recipes));
}
```

Code Explanation

We use the the *ActionName* attribute in the delete method which we did not use for the create and edit methods

```
[HttpPost, ActionName("Delete")]
[ValidateAntiForgeryToken]
public IActionResult DeleteConfirmed(int id)
```

The action name attribute allows us to use a different method name for the URL than the actual method name in the code. For this delete function, even though the method in the code is called *DeleteConfirmed*, we use *ActionName("Delete")* so that the URL looks simpler and just reads **/Delete**. This helps keep URLs clean and easy to understand, while the code can have more specific method names that describe what they do more clearly.

To delete the recipe, we use two methods on the *_context* object: the *Find* method to retrieve the recipe object and, once we have it, pass it to the *Remove* method to be deleted.

```
var recipe = _context.Recipes.Find(id);
if (recipe != null)
{
        _context.Recipes.Remove(recipe);
        _context.SaveChanges();
        TempData["RecipeRemoved"] = recipe.Name;
}
```

We then use this code

```
TempData["RecipeRemoved"] = recipe.Name;
```

We write the recipe name into the *TempData* dictionary because after deleting a recipe, we take the user back to the Recipe search screen. We could have shown the user a short confirmation message and left them to navigate back to the search screen, but I thought taking them back to the search screen would make for a nicer user experience.

The reason why we use the *TempData* dictionary rather than *ViewData* or *ViewBag* functionality that we have looked at previously is that we're calling

```
return RedirectToAction(nameof(Recipes));
```

By calling *RedirectToAction*, we take the user back to the Recipes view. However, because we're redirecting, the data in the *ViewData* and *ViewBag* constructs will be lost. The *TempData* dictionary can persist data between redirects, so it is the ideal choice for this scenario.

We can now also make a change to the Recipes view so that when the user is redirected there, they get a confirmation message saying their chosen recipe has been deleted. Here's the code from the Recipes View with the functionality we've added to display the message in bold

```
@model RecipeDatabase.Models.RecipeSearchViewModel

@{
    ViewBag.Title = "Recipes";
    string searchString = Context.Request.Query["searchString"];
    string recipeRemoved = TempData["RecipeRemoved"] as string ?? string.Empty;

}
<div class="container my-4">
    <h1 class="mb-3">Recipes</h1>

    <!-- Search form -->
    <form method="get" class="form-inline mb-3">
        @if (!string.IsNullOrEmpty(recipeRemoved)) {
            <div  id="removedMessage" class="alert alert-success" role="alert">Recipe "@recipeRemoved" has been removed succesfully</div>
        }
        <div class="form-group mb-2">
            <input type="text" name="searchString" class="form-control" placeholder="Search Recipes" value="@searchString"/>
        </div>
        <div class="form-group mb-2">
            <select class="form-control" asp-items="Model.Categories" name="recipeCategory">
                <option value="">All Categories</option>
            </select>
        </div>
        <button type="submit" class="btn btn-primary">Search</button>
    </form>

    <div class="mb-2">
        @Model.Recipes.Count recipes returned.
    </div>

    <!-- Recipes List -->
    <div class="row">
        @foreach (var recipe in Model.Recipes)
        {
            <div class="col-md-4 mb-4">
                <div class="card h-100">
                    <img class="card-img-top" src="@recipe.ImagePath" alt="@recipe.Name">
                    <div class="card-body d-flex flex-column">
                        <h5 class="card-title">@recipe.Name</h5>
                        <p class="card-text">@recipe.Description</p>
                        <a href="@Url.Action("Recipe", "Recipe", new { id = recipe.Id })" class="btn btn-primary mt-auto">View Recipe</a>
```

```
                    </div>
                </div>
            </div>
        }
    </div>
</div>

@section Scripts {
    <script>
        $(document).ready(function() {
            // Check if the element exists before setting the timeout
            if ($('#removedMessage').length) {
                setTimeout(function() {
                    $('#removedMessage').fadeOut('slow');
                }, 5000); // 5000 milliseconds = 5 seconds
            }
        });
    </script>
}
```

Code Explanation

To see what's happening here, we'll go through the bolded bits of code one by one

```
string recipeRemoved = TempData["RecipeRemoved"] as string ?? string.Empty;
```

Here, we check to see if there is a *RecipeRemoved* value in the *TempData* dictionary. If there is, we assign it to the *recipeRemoved* variable. If there isn't, we set the value of the *recipeRemoved* variable to an empty string.

```
@if (!string.IsNullOrEmpty(recipeRemoved)) {
            <div id="removedMessage" class="alert alert-success" role="alert">Recipe "@recipeRemoved" has been removed successfully</div>
        }
```

Having set the value of the *recipeRemoved* variable, we check it to see if it has a value; if it does contain a value, we output a message to the screen informing the user that the delete has taken place. We use built-in styles from the bootstrapper framework to style the message.

At this point, the functionality is complete in the fact that the user will be informed that the delete has taken place, but to make things a bit nicer from a UI perspective we also add a jQuery function

```
$(document).ready(function() {
        // Check if the element exists before setting the timeout
        if ($('#removedMessage').length) {
            setTimeout(function() {
                $('#removedMessage').fadeOut('slow');
            }, 5000); // 5000 milliseconds = 5 seconds
}
```

The jQuery function checks to see if we've added an updated message to the page by checking to see if an element with the id of *"removedMessage"* exists; if it finds any elements, then it uses the jQuery *fadeout* function to fade the message out of view after 5 seconds have elapsed.

Putting it all together, you can see what the user will see after deleting a recipe in Figure 2

Figure 2 – What the user sees after deleting a recipe

Now that we have the Edit and Delete functionality in place, we'll add a couple of links so that the user can easily edit and delte recipes we'll do this by changing the code in the Recipe.cshtml file in the Views/Recipe folder, I've included the full view code below with the changes in bold

```
@model RecipeDatabase.Models.Recipe
@{
    ViewBag.Title = Model.Name;
}

<div class="container">
    <div class="row">
        <div class="col-md-6">
            <img src="@Model.ImagePath" alt="@Model.Name" class="img-fluid">
        </div>
        <div class="col-md-6">
            <h1>@Model.Name</h1>
            <h4>Category: @Model.Category</h4>
            <hr>
            <h3>Description:</h3>
            <p>@Html.Raw(Model.Description)</p>
            <h3>Instructions:</h3>
            <p>@Html.Raw(Model.RecipeInstructions.Replace("\n","<br>"))</p>

            @Html.ActionLink("Edit This Recipe", "Edit", "Recipe", new { id = @Model.Id }, new { @class = "btn btn-secondary" })
            @Html.ActionLink("Delete This Recipe", "Delete", "Recipe", new { id = @Model.Id }, new { @class = "btn btn-secondary" })

        </div>
    </div>
</div>
```

As you can see from the code, two links have been added using the Razor *@Html.ActionLink* helper method; we pass the recipe ID from the Model into the links so when they are clicked, the user is taken straight to the edit/delete screen for the relevant recipe. You can see the link buttons on display in Figure 3

Pancakes

Category: Breakfast

Description:
Light and fluffy pancakes served with warm maple syrup and fresh berries. A delightful way to start any morning.

Instructions:
1. Whisk together flour, sugar, baking powder, and salt.
2. Add eggs, milk, and melted butter; mix until smooth.
3. Pour batter onto a heated griddle.
4. Cook until bubbles form, then flip and cook other side.
5. Serve hot with syrup and berries.

[Edit This Recipe] [Delete This Recipe]

Figure 3 – The Edit and Delete link buttons on the Recipe edit screen

Chapter 14: Finishing Touches

Now we have all the functionality in place we'll just make a couple of changes to the *_Layout.cshtml* file so users can easily access the functionality we've added. Rather than list the entire file here, I'm just going to show you the changes to the header element, so you can make these changes in your code by removing the header element from your *_Layout.cshtml* file and copying the code below in.

```
<header>
<nav class="navbar navbar-expand-sm navbar-toggleable-sm navbar-light bg-white border-bottom box-shadow mb-3">
        <div class="container-fluid">
            <a class="navbar-brand" asp-area="" asp-controller="Home" asp-action="Index">Recipe Database</a>
            <button class="navbar-toggler" type="button" data-bs-toggle="collapse" data-bs-target=".navbar-collapse" aria-controls="navbarSupportedContent"
                    aria-expanded="false" aria-label="Toggle navigation">
                <span class="navbar-toggler-icon"></span>
            </button>
            <div class="navbar-collapse collapse d-sm-inline-flex justify-content-between">
                <ul class="navbar-nav flex-grow-1">
                    <li class="nav-item">
                        <a class="nav-link text-dark" asp-area="" asp-controller="Home" asp-action="Index">Home</a>
                    </li>
                    <li class="nav-item">
                        <a class="nav-link text-dark" asp-area="" asp-controller="Home" asp-action="Privacy">Privacy</a>
                    </li>
                    <li class="nav-item">
                        <a class="nav-link text-dark" asp-area="" asp-controller="Recipe" asp-action="Recipes">Recipes</a>
                    </li>
                    <li class="nav-item">
                        <a class="nav-link text-dark" asp-area="" asp-controller="Recipe" asp-action="Create">Add Recipe</a>
                    </li>
                </ul>
            </div>
        </div>
</nav>
</header>
```

Once the changes are in place the site header should look like Figure 1

Figure 1 – The updated site header

The Recipes link should take the user to the Recipe search screen, and the Add Recipe link should navigate to the Create Recipe screen.

Chapter 15: Final Word

Our recipe database project is complete! I hope you've enjoyed coding it as much as I've enjoyed guiding you through the process. This experience should provide you with a solid foundation in creating ASP.NET MVC projects, working with databases, and implementing essential features. You can now use these skills as a stepping stone for your future endeavours in web development.

Thank you for following along with this book! ☐ If you have any questions or would just like to share your thoughts and feedback, please don't hesitate to reach out. I'm always here to help and would love to hear from you.

I can be reached at ian@hardworkingnerd.com, which is the same email you should use if you would like me to send you all the source code used in this book. As an extra reward for finishing the book, if you mention in your email that you made it to Chapter 15, then I'll send you an additional extra bonus.

Keep coding, keep learning, and most importantly, have fun! ☐

Made in the USA
Columbia, SC
21 November 2024